July 28, 2002
Sacramento

THE CORN SNAKE MANUAL
Bill Love & Kathy Love

Published by Advanced Vivarium Systems, Inc.

www.avsbooks.com

1-800-982-9410

ACKNOWLEDGEMENTS

We are sincerely grateful to the following individuals, a true brotherhood of corn snake enthusiasts who all answered our calls for help in researching and illustrating this project. The authors alone accept full responsibility for any errors that have crept into this book by our digesting and condensing the information they provided.

Thank you Glenn Abramczyk, Joan Alderson, Nancy Bajek, Brian Barczyk (B.H.B. Enterprises), Andy Barr, Jeff Barringer, Dick & Patti Bartlett, Aaron Bauer, Dr. H. Bernard & Bette Bechtel, Mark & Kim Bell, Bill Brant (The Gourmet Rodent), Jim Bridges, Mark Brown, Fred Burton, Kevin Calvey, Ken Clark, Jack Cole, Stephen & Jennifer Coney, Jon Coote, Jillian Cowles, John Crickmer, John Decker, Jeff Dominguez, Kevin Enge, Bob Ehrig, Dwight Good, Mark Hazel, Adrian Hemens, Joe Hiduke (The Gourmet Rodent), Paul J. Hollander, Sacha Korell, Dr. Shawn Lockhart, Pat & Jerry Loll, Rob MacInnes, Michael J. McEachern *(whose predecessor books from 1991 by Advanced Vivarium Systems were borrowed upon for some data)*, Jim McLean, John Mills, Ryan Moss, Mark Pellicer, Dave Powell, Tim Rainwater (Rainwater Reptiles), Randy Remington, Bill Savary, P. Smith, Rich & Connie Zuchowski (SerpenCo), Adam Song, Noel "Mick" Spencer, Scott J. Stahl DVM, Kevin Stevens (Coast to Coast Exotics), Karen & Joe Street, Stephen Stresser, our daughter Darya Tchetvergova, Craig Trumbower, Bob Wallen, Brent Ward, and Don & Tammie Soderberg (South Mountain Reptiles).

Tidbits of information and ideas were also anonymously sifted from countless pieces of correspondence flowing across *kingsnake.com*'s Corn Snake Forum. We thank the numerous people who've chosen to answer questions and share their knowledge in that relatively new online medium.

Deserving of special thanks for their generous donation of time and expertise in proofreading all or part of this manuscript, and suggesting many factual and grammatical corrections, are: Don Soderberg, Rich Zuchowski, Bern Bechtel, Bill Brant, Joe Hiduke, Scott Stahl DVM, Shawn Lockhart, Tim Rainwater, Kevin Enge, and especially Paul Hollander. Again, any mistakes that slipped in were *ours*. Jim Bridges of Hollywood, Florida also used his extraordinary digital imaging and photographic talents to conjure up the cover of this book from our slides.

Lastly we thank our editors Philippe & Gigi de Vosjoli and Susan Donoghue VMD at Advanced Vivarium Systems for their unflagging faith and enduring patience in seeing this 'simple update' through to publication.

All photos are by the authors unless credited otherwise.

DEDICATION

H. Bernard Bechtel is best known as the creator of the amelanistic corn snake, but his contribution to herpetoculture extends far beyond that narrow accomplishment. His curiosity, professionally carried-out breeding investigations spanning nearly half a century, and his personal enthusiasm almost single-handedly launched the tremendous interest and growth that the hobby is experiencing today. For years he freely donated living specimens, many of which were extremely rare and valuable at the time, to serious researchers and hobbyists alike who wished to study and further investigate the genetics of color and pattern inheritance. This is his nature – to help others add to the pool of knowledge about a subject he feels dearly about. It seems ironic that Bern's contributions have taken place largely in the shadow of the draconian laws of his home state of Georgia – a state which to this day still forbids commerce in captive-bred offspring of a common native species that is also the dominant snake in world herpetoculture today.

We both are fortunate to have been frequent recipients of his generosity with specimens and knowledge, and are honored to recognize his lifetime achievements by dedicating this volume to him.

The Corn Snake Manual
Table of Contents

INTRODUCTION

"What is the best kind of pet snake in the entire world?" Ideally, the answer must be a type that meets the following criteria: 1) has a calm disposition around people, i.e. it isn't prone to biting, constricting, or defecating under mild stress; 2) has an attractive appearance to humans; 3) is a convenient size to handle and enjoy as a pet; 4) has space, climate, and food requirements that are easy to provide in captivity; 5) does not pose a physical danger to people; 6) is easy to induce to reproduce and raise offspring; and 7) is genetically variable to stimulate continued fascination and expansion of interest in herpetoculture.

Corn snakes pass all these tests admirably. More *Elaphe guttata* are bred in captivity each year than any other species of snake on Earth, resulting in offspring that supply the vast majority of specimens available in the pet trade today. Their current prevalence as the world's #1 pet serpent species is having negligible impact on wild corn snake populations, an important factor as myriad other organisms are declining due to the pressure of mankind's domination of the planet.

The intended audience for this book spans everyone from the novice needing the basics of feeding and housing care to the seasoned veteran of corn herpetoculture who wants to know the latest on breeding, genetics, and range and history of color and pattern variations. We, the authors, have put everything we know into making this the most comprehensive publication on the subject of keeping and breeding corn snakes available.

Bette and Bern Bechtel in the snake room of their home in November 1978.

PART I GENERAL INFORMATION AND HUSBANDRY

WHAT IS A CORN SNAKE?

Corns are members of the large common snake family Colubridae, which includes the kings, milks, bulls, pines, garters, waters, and racers. Scientifically known as the species *Elaphe guttata*, they share the first part of their Latin name (genus) with such familiar relatives as the black, grey, yellow, and Texas rat snakes (all races of *Elaphe obsoleta*) and fox snakes *Elaphe vulpina*. Corn snakes are medium-sized, non-venomous constrictors that prefer to be active around dusk and early evening in habitats ranging from fields to woodlands across the southern and east central United States. Their vernacular name was coined from their habit of frequenting the vicinities of storage structures for corn. Such places are often the breeding sites of abundant rodents, their principal prey as adults. Indeed, this species thrives in close association with man's interspersed farming regions where an abundance of vermin typically thrives along the overgrown edge zones. People who collect snakes commercially have suggested that because of this widespread modern land use practice, corns may be more common per acre, at least in some heavily agriculturalized regions, than they have ever been in history.

The resemblance of the checkered ventral pattern to multi-colored Indian corn has also been noted as a possible source for the corn snake's vernacular name. 'Red rat snake' is used quite appropriately too, although some people retain this name for only the nominate subspecies *E. guttata guttata*. This eastern U.S. population ranges from south-central New Jersey's Pine Barrens in the northeasternmost edge of its natural range, west to the vicinity of Reelfoot Lake in northwestern Tennessee, and south to the Atchafalaya Basin of southern Louisiana. Corn snakes live in areas to the southeast of lines connecting these points, including many of the offshore islands. Stowaways in exotic plants exported from southern Florida are likely the source of its introduction and establishment on Grand Cayman in the Caribbean and New Providence Island, Nassau in the Bahamas.

Only one other official subspecies exists - the **Emory's** or **Great Plains rat snake** *Elaphe guttata emoryi* from the south central U.S. and northeastern Mexico, including most of Texas, Oklahoma, Kansas, and parts of the surrounding states. Some taxonomists are currently claiming that *emoryi* should be elevated to a full species. In 1994, the subspecific name *meahllmorum* had been proposed for populations at the southeastern end of the present *emoryi* range to further split that subspecies (or species), though it hasn't been widely accepted at this time. The same applies to the isolated, far-western U.S. race of *guttata* occurring in eastern Utah and western Colorado that has sometimes been referred to by the subspecific name *intermontanus*. The western races of *guttata* have not generally proven to be as popular in captivity as the eastern subspecies so far, primarily because of their duller, tannish-grey earthy tones.

The name **rosy rat snake** *E. g. rosacea* appears in older literature and refers to generally smaller and paler populations of corns on the lower Florida Keys. Reigning taxonomists designate it as merely a local race in recent literature. The snakes exhibit variation ranging from grey or straw yellow backgrounds with dull orange or brownish blotches to some approaching the red on red-oranges of typical mainland corns. It's possible for an experienced field collector to make an educated guess as to the insular origin of some animals by appearance alone, although this is by no means a foolproof method.

The Great Plains rat snake *Elaphe guttata emoryi* is generally more subdued in coloration than its eastern relatives. This one is from western Texas near the Mexican border.

ACQUIRING A CORN SNAKE

What do you look for in determining a new snake's health? While it's not possible to completely guarantee a problem-free snake by examining its external appearance, look for these signs:

Alertness and Attentiveness. The snake should move deliberately, yet cautiously, flicking its tongue often to check all new environmental stimuli when held or exploring.

Body Weight. A cross-section view of a healthy corn snake should resemble a loaf of bread, without loose folds of skin or ribs protruding, and without a backbone ridge standing out. The belly scutes should be fairly flat and "squared off" from the sides of the body.

Muscle Tone. The snake should feel strong and be able to resist somewhat if you manipulate its body with your fingers. Check for 'mushy' bellies and rear ends. Listless, weak specimens are always a poor acquisition risk.

Stool Appearance. Stools should consist of solid brownish-black masses along with some yellowish semi-solids or viscous fluids, and maybe a little clearish fluid too. Strange colors like greens or blues, blood in any form, an overly jelly-like, waxy, or mushy mass, or half or more of the estimated weight represented by liquids are all signs of problems.

Defects and Scars. Avoid a snake with odd lumps, body kinks, or indentations that may indicate a serious old injury or genetic abnormality. The best way to check for these is to run the entire length

These three specimens demonstrate some of the range of color variation among the race of corns formerly known as rosy rats *Elaphe guttata rosacea* from the Florida Keys. *Photo by Joan Alderson.*

of its body through your lightly closed hands to feel for irregularities. Small tail kinks alone probably won't be detrimental in a pet, but snakes with such conditions shouldn't be used for breeding. The eyes should look clear (assuming that the snake is not about to shed). The cloaca should close tightly and be dry. Patches of unshed skin may be indications of other problems, but are relatively harmless in themselves if they don't involve the underlying skin. The potential difficulty in treating open skin/scale infections or scrapes should be judged much as you would for comparable injuries on your own body. Old surface scars won't affect overall health or breeding, only detract from the animal's beauty.

Respiratory Infections. Listen to the snake's breathing for any hint of whistling or gurgling, and look for liquids or bubbles coming from the nostrils or mouth. These could indicate a respiratory infection, which you don't want to start with in a new pet. The mouth should close snugly and have no signs of sores, scabs, or bleeding of any kind, which may be precursors of, or lead to, mouthrot.

External Parasites. Look for "bugs" attached anywhere on the snake's body. Mites are your biggest worry. They're usually red or black, and tiny, like coarse pepper granules, and either cram between scales or wander slowly over the body. They harm their hosts by sucking blood, which may amount to significant volumes if a large infestation exists, or if the snake is very small. They also may transmit diseases, especially if coming from a source where many other herps are housed. Look for them tucked beneath the edges of the scales bordering the eyes, in the mental groove (under the middle of the chin), or on your hands after letting the snake forcibly slide through them.

Ticks are generally larger (1/16 to 1/4 inch), flat, "scale-like" bloodsuckers that hold on by their mouths. They're rare on corns, and alone are not considered to be an insurmountable obstacle to the new snake owner.

OTHER TIPS FOR CHOOSING A NEW CORN SNAKE

You may wish to find out if a specimen feeds voluntarily, and on what types of prey items, by asking the seller about its history. Snakes accustomed to accepting newborn mice, especially prekilled thawed ones, are the handiest to obtain food for in most situations. If you're at the breeder's or seller's location, consider asking to test a baby corn by offering it food while you watch. You may not want to let it actually consume the meal if you'll be traveling with it soon, only see that it makes an attempt to eat on its own. Don't be too disappointed if it doesn't feed on command though - it may simply be nervous or not hungry during the moment of your test.

The snake's individual temperament may also be assessed at this time by direct handling. Keep in mind that juveniles are typically more nervous than adults. It's normal for hatchlings to defend themselves against a large, formidable object like your approaching hand. This kind of aggression is normal and should fade quickly as they mature and learn to trust that you're not a threat to them. Adult corns virtually always have a calm demeanor, although certain rare individuals may be high-strung and nippy when first held. We have noted that when the scent of food is fresh in the air, corns may lunge for hands in mistaken excitement to grab the first moving object they see. They also have a flighty reaction if the lingering aroma of the last king snake (genus *Lampropeltis*) you touched is detected on your hands.

By buying a juvenile as opposed to an adult, you often have the choice of a greater variety in colors and patterns. You will also know its approximate age and have the chance to learn some past history, like viewing the parental stock, from the vendor. These are facts that may be valuable to your future breeding plans. You'll get to see the colors blossom out on a growing juvenile and enjoy its youthful vibrancy during the first several years of life when most corns look their absolute best. Youngsters take up less space than adults, making them easier to start in plastic shoeboxes or other small cages. Relatively fewer baby corns are collected from the wild anymore, so it will *probably* also be captive-bred, as are most young snakes found in the pet trade nowadays. This means it's more likely to adapt to captivity easily and will be less likely to be parasitized than a wild-caught snake.

Buying a hatchling has some disadvantages. These relatively fragile little creatures become stressed by too much attention and handling, especially by young children. This may cause them to be shy feeders or to regurgitate meals more readily within a few days of ingesting them. A low percentage of baby corns stubbornly refuse certain kinds of foods that are convenient for humans to offer, such as pinkie mice. When they are feeding and digesting meals normally, they can easily consume two to three times the number of individual items that would satisfy adults. Bi-weekly feedings are not a necessity but will promote rapid growth if you can afford the time and money to feed them this way. Corns mature rapidly, often in two years or less, so waiting to raise an adult shouldn't take long and is well worth the wait of starting with a baby specimen.

Older corns are big and impressive, although their colors are often duller and darker than young adults. Healthy-looking adults may be found for sale for many reasons, but as with used cars, beware of hidden flaws such as reproductive failure. A husky five-foot long corn may appear to be an 'instant breeder' sizewise, but that should make you at least consider why it was not kept for breeding by the person who raised it. The one thing you can usually count on is that it doesn't have a temperament problem. Corn snakes have individual personalities, but as a rule of thumb, the species is extraordinarily mild-natured at all sizes and ages. If by chance you encounter an exception to this rule though, don't expect a very big old animal to necessarily change radically and become tame with gentle handling and patience.

SOURCES FOR CORN SNAKES

Corn snakes are either collected from the wild or bred in captivity. *Elaphe guttata* is not considered threatened in nature, except possibly in some isolated pockets, on very small islands that are utilized intensively by man, or on the periphery of their range. However, they are protected by law in certain states in which they occur such as Georgia and New Jersey. Wild specimens are gentle as a rule, adapt readily to captivity, and can make excellent pets. On the other hand, they *may* be finicky feeders, and may have scars or other imperfections, less-than-ideal coloration, or hidden diseases and/or parasites.

Field-collected specimens in the 18–30 inch (46–76 cm) size range adapt best to captivity. They are beyond the slightly delicate baby stage, yet not so old and "set in their ways" that adjusting to a captive environment is too stressful. When considering captive-bred stock without the benefit of any background history, another advantage of acquiring specimens in that size range is that they are still too young to be someone's 'rejects' due to breeding problems.

Captive-bred specimens are easy to find. Most towns and cities have pet shops that stock herps. Mail-order breeders and dealers have ads in herp publications and on the Internet. When choosing a dealer to buy from, discuss the health aspects listed above by phone to assure yourself of their knowledge and honesty. Ask how long he or she has been in business, and ask about references from recent satisfied customers. When feasible, choose your animals directly from a breeder in your area at his place of business. Nothing beats selecting your corns in person where you can examine them carefully, see their parents and siblings for comparisons, and ask any pertinent questions at length. Besides ascertaining their health, you may personally double check sexes* (*more on this later). Swap shows can also be good sources for corn snakes as these events often seem to ooze with great animals at bargain prices. But if buying from hobbyist breeders, especially non-local hobbyists rather than dealers or breeders in business year-round, be aware that they may not be around to answer questions or help with problems after the show is over.

TRANSPORTATION and SHIPPING

Any corn snake can be transported individually inside one of two types of containers that have become standards in the industry. Juveniles fit nicely inside plastic delicatessen food cups and tubs with snap-on lids and multiple air holes in the sides. Cloth sacks or sturdy pillow cases work best for specimens over approximately 18 inches (46 cm) in length.

When packing snakes for shipping, stuff crushed newspaper around the cups or sacks so they can't bounce around inside the shipping box. A styrofoam-lined, heavy cardboard box (as is standard for the tropical fish industry) offers temporary protection against harmful outdoor temperature fluctuations that might otherwise overheat or chill sensitive herps during transit. Chemical reaction-triggered heat packs or frozen cold packs can be placed inside the box to help maintain a more stable temperature. Care must be taken to provide adequate ventilation because heat packs consume oxygen in the warming process.

Air freight between airports has been the old reliable method of transport for years, and now some large parcel services also accept live harmless snakes IF packaged according to their escape-proof standards. Check with them for details. The U.S. Postal Service does NOT accept live snakes for mailing.

LEGALITIES

Today we live with more laws than anyone can hope to know or even be fully aware of. These regulations are frequently ill-conceived in haste by people who fear or hate reptiles. We herpers must stay aware of a plethora of constantly changing regulations that may directly or indirectly affect our freedom to interact with corn snakes and other herps, even in the privacy of our own homes. When laws concern herps, they're usually aimed at one of three different aspects: 1) protecting endangered species; 2) keeping species away which might escape and become problems should they breed and become established in the area; and 3) avoiding having species within certain communities' jurisdictions that might frighten or injure people. Corns seldom realistically fit any of these descriptions, but don't be too surprised when they're swept into one or more of these categories by virtue of being considered wildlife, non-native to your area, or simply because they're snakes.

When laws do apply, getting caught disobeying them, whether or not they seem to make any sense to you, will cause you headaches best avoided if possible. It's wise to check with both your home town's zoning department and state wildlife department about any laws that may affect the keeping of corn snakes in your area. Let our hand of experience guide you, especially with smaller local authorities, when we suggest calling anonymously, asking for the name and position of whoever speaks to you, and requesting reference numbers of any regulations they quote. This may help keep them honest when the tendency is often strong to simply say "No!" and make the perceived nasty problem go away. Libraries usually also have sets of municipal ordinances in their reference collection where you may check on local laws that pertain to animals.

ACCLIMATION

Shipping via any method is a long, bumpy ride and a somewhat traumatic experience for animals. This is especially true for babies, so the following advice is particularly applicable to them. Have a suitable cage ready to set them up in with the basics in place – a shelter for hiding and a container of clean water. Newspaper makes a good initial cage substrate so anything shed or excreted can be found easily for examination. Setting the cage in a place that receives a natural photoperiod of day versus night helps animals' biological clocks function on regular schedules. Do not, however, put it in full direct sunlight which could quickly overheat a closed-in cage or aquarium. The best thing you can do is *leave them alone for a minimum of three full days and nights!* Let them settle down in their new surroundings. Their whole universe has just been changed, and they're nervous. Wait until the fourth day to give them a smallish meal as a test; then proceed with a normal feeding routine after the first meal has been assimilated completely without problems.

QUARANTINE

Every new specimen is a possible source of disease and parasites that can spread through an established collection. The best preventative medicine you can provide is to isolate a new specimen from the rest of your herps, ideally in a totally separate room for at least one shedding cycle, as a smart precaution. During that period, which is seldom more than a couple of months, keep inspecting the new specimen for all the problems outlined above. Some breeders advise that six months is the minimum time to quarantine new specimens and thoroughly check them out, especially as it pertains to screening for *Cryptosporidium* (see INTERNAL PARASITES). Wash your hands thoroughly before touching any other animals, preferably in a solution of one part liquid chlorine bleach to nine parts water, or with a germicidal soap. In addition, attend to the quarantine room *after* finishing the regular maintenance of the rest of your collection.

If you have any reason to suspect a parasite problem, or even if you don't and simply wish to play it safe, this is also a good time to get a stool sample from the new snake to a veterinarian for examination. Parasites don't necessarily have to be identified down to the individual species level; the general type alone (e.g. roundworms, tapeworms, etc.) is usually enough to determine appropriate treatment. A willing cat and dog vet should be able to perform a basic fecal exam, but not all vets will work on, or are even familiar with, herps. (You may have to search a bit to find a herp vet in your region: see ARAV in the appendix for help with this.) If all else fails, many tests may be performed by sending samples via the mail to qualified vets located out of state. One way or another, however, consult a specialist herp vet before the actual treatment commences. An inexperienced vet might be tempted to use mammalian dosages of drugs, which are usually too high for herps.

BASIC CAGING REQUIREMENTS

Escaped snakes are a primary cause of legislation that restricts their ownership so getting an escape-proof enclosure must be a primary consideration when purchasing or building a snake enclosure. The most readily available are the all-glass reptile enclosures with sliding screen tops now sold in many pet stores. Most have a pin type of locking mechanism. The minimum size enclosure for a single adult corn snake is a standard 20 gallon tank (12L x 30W x 12H inches (30 x 76 x 30 cm). Larger enclosures are preferable and will allow your snakes to roam and exercise. For better monitoring, hatchlings are best started in a large plastic terrarium or ten-gallon sliding screened-top enclosure before graduation to a larger cage.

When building your own larger cage, the material used for the walls should have a smooth, non-porous surface for easy cleaning and sterilization. Glass works best, though plexiglas, fiberglass, aluminum, or sealed wood is also satisfactory. The most important point is that cracks and gaps are narrow enough to prevent a snake from squeezing its snout within the tight space as it searches for an escape route. Crevices along the lowest several inches are especially important to seal to prevent spilled fluids or liquid excreta from seeping in and allowing bacteria to collect and grow. Make sure that all sealants or paints are thoroughly cured so toxic fumes aren't inhaled by the cage occupant.

If the entire top isn't ventilated (as a full screen terrarium lid is), at least two separate openings of four square inches (34 cm^2) (minimally) should be present on different sides of the cage for air exchange. Preferably one opening should be lower and one higher to encourage cross-ventilation in the slightest breeze or room thermocline. The mesh covering the openings should have individual holes no larger than 1/8 inch (3 mm) and should present a non-abrasive surface when your fingers are dragged across it firmly. If the mesh feels rough, your snake may rub its snout raw against it.

One-piece molded plastic glass-fronted herp cages of all sizes have become fashionable in recent years. Myriad designs offer access from front removable sliding glass or rear ceiling hatches, and with all manner of ventilation and light openings too. Their smooth insides are easily cleaned and sterilized. Some kinds are square in profile so many similar units are stackable, although the cost quickly becomes prohibitive compared to many herpers' utilization of other prefabricated storage boxes on the mass market today.

Hatchlings are most easily housed in clear or translucent plastic storage boxes with close-fitting lids. These are often marketed in store houseware departments as shoeboxes. Holes of no larger than 1/8 inch (3 mm) in diameter can be melted or drilled into each of the four sides along the upper edges. The number of holes should vary according to whether you're trying to retain moisture (if you live in a dry desert climate) or trying to let the cage air out (where high relative humidity prevails, as in Florida).

Plastic boxes fit nicely into specially-built shelving units in which each overhead shelf is less than 1/4 inch above the lid of the unit below it. The low overhead prevents the box lid from rising far enough to let the occupant escape. Other systems designed with closer tolerances use larger boxes without lids at all; the shelf bottom above acts as the lid to the cage below. The shallower kinds of units minimize unnecessary vertical space to allow more actual cages in a smaller area. Since the units are not meant to show off specimens, the dim light coming into them isn't important for viewing. And the snakes may feel more secure in the dim light with a minimum number of disturbances in such a system. These high-rise styles of economical housing were first developed by private commercial breeders of colubrid snakes so they could maintain large numbers of specimens in their ongoing projects. Attractive professional models are now mass-produced and sold for carpenterially-challenged herpetoculturists. Popular herp magazines are a great source of ads for such specialty units.

LOST AND FOUND

No matter what style of containment system is utilized, a tight-fitting door, heavily weighted-down lid, or other method of securely closing it is mandatory to prevent escapes. Corn snakes' climbing agility and expertise at squeezing out of tiny cracks and openings is nearly legendary. Whenever they do escape, they seem to remember how they managed it the first time. The next occurrence will take place in one-tenth the time it took the snake to figure it out the last time if you don't correct the situation immediately. When corns occasionally do find their way out of their cage, their dash to freedom is often anything but fast or calculated. They usually explore upward, so seeking them on or inside things on shelves, clinging around window casings, on blinds or curtain rods, behind wall pictures, in hanging plants, etc. is a wise recovery tactic. They will eventually take to the floor and follow the room's perimeter until stumbling upon a doorway or crevice along the wall. A clever snake trap device that addresses this habit is built and sold by BJ Specialties, Boerne, Texas specifically for collectors faced with this dilemma. It works on the same principal as a funnel trap for fish by tempting a roaming snake to wander into the dark retreat it offers when encountered along an otherwise open stretch of wall.

NUMBER OF SNAKES PER ENCLOSURE

Housing corns individually, except of course during breeding efforts, is the time-honored method for observation. Separation ensures getting to know the personality of each specimen in your care and being able to make suitable husbandry adjustments to help them along. You can also keep track of and record shedding and other life functions when you don't have to guess which of multiple cage inhabitants is responsible for leaving each clue. Additionally, if two (or more) cagemates cohabitate, feeding must be closely monitored to eliminate competition over single food items. If fed together, two snakes will almost invariably seize the same prey, even with multiple choices in front of their noses. As they engulf the prey from each end, the snake whose bite first covers the snout of the other may continue to swallow its cagemate. The extremely rare instances of cannibalism in captive *Elaphe guttata* can usually be traced to this phenomenon.

Other times, one corn of a pair may be shy and intimidated, becoming a poor or sporadic feeder faced with the fiercer competition of an aggressive cagemate. Using a temporary shift cage, which can be as simple as a clean empty garbage can, is a handy way to separate a pair of corns during feeding that otherwise live together in harmony. Gently lift the snake that usually grabs the food item first and put it into the can, since it's probably the more adventurous and less distracted feeder of the pair. There it can eat in peace while also reducing the risk of it, or any specimen prone to such tendencies, from accidentally swallowing any loose cage substrate materials. Watch out when reintroducing it back with its cagemate since the residual aroma of the prey on one snake's body could elicit a feeding strike from the other.

SUBSTRATES

A good cage substrate should 1) absorb fecal material and stop it from spreading very far, 2) cover the cage floor to give the snake traction for movement, and 3) be visually appealing. Newspaper can work temporarily, but tends to get folded over as the snake explores beneath it. Newspaper isn't pretty, but it's cheap and easy to change when soiled. Indoor-outdoor carpeting such as Astroturf™ looks a little better, but traps moisture below it, causing smells to linger and bacteria to grow.

Flexible plastic storage tubs that slide into custom-built racks without the need of separate lids make convenient caging systems for housing large numbers of corns for breeding.

It also takes a long time to dry thoroughly after washing and disinfecting.

A substrate material should cover the tank floor to a depth of one to two inches (2.5–5 cm). Wood chips or wood fibers are the substrates of choice in the U.S. today. Depending upon the type, they also provide ample traction for crawling. Aspen bedding is a pale shredded wood fiber with little dust or scent that works particularly well for this. It's an absorbent substance that clumps together well when defecations land on it, keeping feces concentrated for easy scooping and removal. Aspen's interwoven nature also allows corns to tunnel through it while exploring, and provides them hiding places in the 'caves' formed under it. This can be especially helpful for shy specimens that like to stay out of sight much of the time. Cypress mulch, common in the southern U.S., also works well. Avoid resinous woods such as cedar, pine, and walnut that may be toxic, especially to juveniles or animals in cages with low ventilation.

SHELTERS/HIDE BOXES

Elaphe guttata is shy by nature, spending the vast majority of time tucked out of sight in tree holes and crevices, animal burrows, under debris, in the walls and roofs of old buildings, etc. This is a clue that providing a similar place of concealment in their enclosure is essential for their psychological health. The hiding place will ideally allow the snake's entire body inside but *not* be large enough for an additional snake of the same size to fit inside it too. Corns like to squeeze into tight dark places in order to feel secure from predators while they're

A simple plastic water bowl that's hollow underneath can double as a hiding place for small snakes by adding an access notch in the side.

digesting food, in a shedding cycle, gravid, or just resting. A piece of wrinkled newspaper may suffice, although a shelter that's heavy enough to stay immobilized so it doesn't slide or tip over is often preferable. When a suitable choice is offered, your snake may spend the vast majority of its time comfortably concealed. If you weren't already aware of it, corn snakes lead rather boring lives by human standards. They rarely leave their lairs to prowl on display to the whole world except for particular reasons like sating hunger, seeking mates, etc. Juveniles are more secretive than adults.

Many common containers will serve as a hide box as long as you make an opening that's a little bigger around than the thickest part of the resident snake's body when distended by a meal. Plastic margarine tubs, cardboard boxes, hollow or concave pieces of wood, or any number of creative custom products, manufactured specifically for this purpose, will work. Plastic designs are easier to clean than paper or wood, but cardboard boxes are free and disposable when soiled. If rock piles are chosen, be careful to stack them securely so they can't topple and pin or crush a pet accidentally.

Hanging the hidebox from a wall or ceiling additionally keeps it up off the substrate to make removing feces on the cage floor simpler. A long slender shelter, such as a hollow log sliced in half lengthwise, can provide the added bonus of a temperature range by extending across a portion of the cage under a heat lamp or over a heat tape or pad. This lets the snake avoid stress by being able to choose its preferred digestion temperature without having to bask in the open with a meal distending its stomach. Two hiding places, one at each end of the cage, may also achieve this advantage.

Three basic items needed in all cages are 1) substrate such as wood chips, 2) a small but heavy water bowl, and 3) a place for the occupant to hide and feel secure.

WATER/HUMIDITY

Because corns inhabit the more humid southeastern U.S., they have higher moisture requirements than comparably sized desert species such as western gopher snakes (genus *Pituophis*). The lower relative humidity even inside typical homes in such climates may cause incomplete shedding or dehydration problems that are not suspected at first. This can be a major problem for juvenile corn snakes in particular since they are much more prone to desiccation than adults. In these cases, it may be necessary to provide a slightly moister environment within the cage. This is easily done by

Clear styrene storage boxes sold for shoes make ideal handy cages for juvenile corns up to about a year in age. They can also be adapted for use in rack systems that negate the need for separate lids on each box. Note the disposable 4 oz. food portion cup for water nested inside a retainer made from a 3 inch PVC pipe section glued to the shoebox floor.

covering most of the main ventilation areas of the cage to reduce moisture loss by evaporation. Newspaper laid on top of a screen aquarium lid may be enough to do the trick, or you may need sheet plastic held down by tape, with only a few air holes, to hold water vapor in more thoroughly. The dryness of your climate will dictate your method, or whether additional periodic misting with a spray bottle is necessary. Even living in a non-arid zone may present dryness-related problems if air conditioning or winter heating tend to severely dehumidify the air where your corns are kept.

The amount of time the snake spends coiled inside its hidebox to retain or absorb moisture will help you evaluate the degree of discomfort it's experiencing without shelter. Monitor for skin blisters more frequently than usual when increasing humidity artificially during these times of temporary necessity. A small, three to six inch (8–15 cm) diameter, sturdy water bowl is all that's required by healthy corn snakes. A larger soaking pan can be added temporarily only if deemed necessary during difficulty in shedding. Placement of all water containers should be central in the enclosure since most defecations are left along cage perimeters where the snakes crawl most often.

Splurge and buy two identical water bowls which lack the extended rims that snakes may lift with their coils and spill. The solid types without hollow spaces underneath are heavier and stay in place best. The water *and* the bowl should be replaced every three days to prevent a build-up of harmful bacteria. The water doesn't have to look dirty to be unhealthy! Set the newly removed and rinsed bowl upside-down to dry while it's not in use. Periodically soak all bowls for at least ten minutes in a strong bleach solution to prevent germs from accumulating on the surfaces.

NATURALISTIC DISPLAYS

To turn a basic terrarium into a truly beautiful display vivarium for your home, decorate it with live plants to add a natural element that's appreciated by all. Sturdy plants that thrive in low light indoor situations tend not to be types that might grow in corn snakes' home ranges, but their dash of greenery still throws life into an otherwise drab setting of logs and stones. Aloes, bromeliads, and snake plants (*Sansevieria*) are durable types that can withstand repeatedly being crawled over by adult corns better than most. Keep them potted and away from cage perimeters and corners to avoid crushing by wandering or hiding snakes. For continued health, rotate them regularly with stand-ins so the plants receive some natural light during the in-between times. Ubiquitous *Pothos* is a spreading vine that may be grown directly in the enclosure and allowed to spread since it's hardy enough to survive in most home environments.

HEATING AND LIGHTING

Corns thrive at temperatures in the same range that humans find to be comfortable. This means approximately a range of 70-88°F (21-31°C). But unlike humans with self-regulating body temperatures, snakes can't sustain all bodily functions if kept at any one temperature constantly. There are times when they must experience higher or lower temperatures to facilitate natural functions such as digestion, embryo development, parasite or infection control, or spermatogenesis. Undoubtedly there are reasons for which corn snakes thermoregulate which we don't yet understand. Thermoregulation is the process by which animals purposely move in and out of areas of higher or lower heat to optimize their body temperatures. In nature the sun is the ultimate source of heat, either directly or indirectly (by warming other surfaces). Snakes seek that warmth when they need it and can count on that option on most days of the year. Denying this vital freedom to them is surely an important factor behind many of the health problems that arise in the often-restrictive atmosphere of captivity.

The most popular method of offering heat to a limited portion of a cage is through a heating device under one end of it. Heat tapes are sold which are normally used for warming the soil to help seeds germinate early or to wrap around outdoor water pipes in northern climates to prevent them from freezing. Herpers typically run a length of heat tape along the rear edge of a shelf so many cages can benefit from hot spots where the ends of each enclosure rest over it. The thermostats that are usually built into such units are useless because they only turn the heat on when the temperature gets down to near freezing. All models we've seen work better with the factory thermostat, if present, disengaged. A

Using a flat heat tape under just one end of the cage provides a warm area for the choice of an optimal temperature for digestion. The long hiding "cave", made from a halved paper towel roll, allows the snake to remain hidden while also choosing its preferred comfort zone in relation to the heat.

separate thermostat is then rigged up that reacts to less severe lows, rather than left to heat constantly day and night.

Modern herpetoculturists' lives have been made much easier by new thermostat control units made specially for herps' needs. Excellent units that can accurately monitor and regulate any kind of temperature altering electrical device are available today, taking much of the guesswork out of the situation. These, combined with slender heat pads that barely take up space anchored beneath cage bottoms or under the interior substrate, have greatly simplified and reduced the fire and shock risks of providing heat. Again, check the herp magazine ads for models and sources.

Spotlights or hooded reflectors may also be used to direct incandescent light to a special basking rock or branch that the snake can utilize easily. Be sure that such a source of radiant heat is aimed at only one end of the cage so a cooler and darker retreat exists at the far end. The basking temperature on the perch site directly under the lamp should be approximately 95° F. This slightly "too hot" spot allows the snake to thermoregulate properly to reach the temperatures it desires or needs, but also lets it move away from it when warm enough just as it would do in sunlight.

LIGHTING

Besides lights for heat, you may wish to illuminate the entire enclosure in a tone of light that beautifies the interior and the inhabitant(s). Corn snakes' colors look best under the same kinds of daylight-simulating (or *enhancing*) fluorescent bulbs that have brightened fish aquariums for years. Some brands advertise that they give off limited amounts of UV (ultraviolet) light, which benefits many life forms. The UV they emit seems inconsequential to healthy snakes' well-being as far as has been determined to date, but it doesn't seem to hurt either. It *could* be of benefit to problematical or sick animals if they're able to get very close, 24 inches (61 cm) or less, to it. Based on current information, our best advice is for you to use whichever brand produces the most eye-pleasing results in your display while also aiming for the highest CRI (color rendering index) value obtainable among your favorite bulb choices.

Joseph Laszlo, a pioneer herp breeder in the zoo world whose early experiments with Vita-Lites® were pivotal in herpetocultural progress, felt that herps act more naturally when the color spectrum of light they live under closely mimics the sun. We concur that this makes them 'happier' and strive to make the maximum use of the sun's lighting whenever feasible. The obviously elite choice is allowing unfiltered sunlight to bathe your snake's cage for both a warm basking site and best color rendition, as long as a significant portion is shaded to prevent heat build-up from a miniature greenhouse effect within the cage. Barring the ability to do this, using non-tinted skylights in your herp room is an admirable next-best option. Clear diffusers hanging just below skylights can help spread sunlight over the room, and also prevent it from shining directly onto any cage and baking it.

FEEDING

Corn snakes are strict carnivores, capturing and swallowing whole food animals in the wild. Struggling prey is subdued by constriction, a process by which coils of the snake's body are wrapped around the animal in ever-tightening loops until inhalation, heartbeats, and circulation become impossible. Death usually occurs within two minutes for mammals and birds, occasionally slightly longer for cold-blooded prey. Juvenile corns readily accept treefrogs, small lizards such as anoles and "house" geckos, and newborn rodents among other things. Specimens over three feet (.9 m) in length feed almost exclusively on warm-blooded prey. These food items are normally sought during evenings and at night, though corns may be active at any hour of the day or night when weather conditions are favorable. The norm is for them to consume large meals relative to their body size and then conceal themselves for several days while digestion takes place. The first defecation from the most recent meal comes two to four days later, depending on temperature, at which point the snake is often interested in eating again. It's not necessary to feed corns immediately after they defecate; in nature they might easily spend the next week in search of food items, receiving plenty of exercise in the process.

A newborn pinkie mouse, or at least one that's less than five days old, is enough of a meal for a 12-inch (30 cm) youngster. Just lay it in the cage near wherever the snake is presently hiding, preferably without disturbing the snake in the process. Under ideal digestive conditions – those in which the snake can warm up to 90°F (32°C) over or under a hot spot at its own discretion – you can push it to two pinkies. Offer them one at a time so as not to frighten or confuse the snake with multiple squirming food items. If the snake regurgitates, go back to one smaller item per meal for awhile, and then work up to larger things slowly again a couple weeks later. You can skimp by and offer one pinkie every two weeks and see modest growth, but you won't raise any monsters on this regimen. Baby snakes will eat twice per week, or even occasionally three times per week, if food is offered, growing rapidly to adulthood in under two years at that rate.

Prolonged exposure to unvarying temperatures under about 72°F (22°C) and over 90°F (32°C) should be avoided since regurgitation of partially digested food items often results. Disturbances to snakes with actively digesting meals in their stomachs and intestines should be minimized until the first main feces appear in the cage. This is especially true when more than two food items are eaten or when an exceptionally large meal distends the snake's profile to twice or more its normal diameter anywhere along its length.

FEEDING SCHEDULE

We'd estimate that a very average feeding schedule in captivity for older corns – those 1 ½ to 2 feet (46-61 cm) or longer - might be one or two appropriate-sized food animals every seven to 14 days. One old

Corn snakes are best offered rodents that are approximately 1-1.5 times the diameter of the thickest part of their body. This specimen is engulfing a young rat that's at the upper end of the suitable size range.

adult (retired breeder) mouse, two young sub-adult mice, or one barely weaned rat makes a perfect single meal for an average adult 4 ½-5 foot (137-152 cm) long corn. The recommended rule of thumb we use to gauge correct size of food animals is to try to select ones (ignoring the prey's fur or feather fluffiness in your estimate) that don't exceed one and one-half times the girth of the snake's midbody. A corn can handle even more prodigious single meals if all other aspects of the cage environment are ideally suited to let it thermoregulate and digest its food efficiently. Because of the greater surface area to mass ratio of small items, it's often wiser to give two or more smaller food items rather than a single, huge, hard-to-digest one. Providing a hot spot in the cage so snakes can choose their optimum digestion temperature on a free will basis takes the guesswork away from you and puts it into the "hands" of the real experts – the snakes themselves.

Corn snakes' skin is stretchier than that of milk and king snakes (*Lampropeltis* sp.), but they are less able to swallow huge meals than boas, pythons, and even their rat snake relatives of the species *E. obsoleta*. It's easy to understand that a corn snake lucky enough to find an adult rat or bird in a tree on any given evening's foray could not afford to pass it by, even if it was bigger than the snake might prefer to capture and swallow. This logically means that being physically geared for handling large single food lumps would be a wise strategy. Yet *guttata* is semi-terrestrial in habit, so an occasional discovery of a nest of multiple baby rodents or birds is also a distinct likelihood. In such circumstances, corn snakes are fully prepared to gorge themselves on the entire brood.

FEEDING BEHAVIOR

Ideal temperature conditions for corns to hunt and feed are typically in the mid 70s°F (24°C) to high 80s°F (31°C). An hour before and after dusk with moderate to high humidity is a favored activity time, which is one more variable to consider when faced with a stubborn feeder in captivity. A corn will slowly wander out of its resting abode and actively flick its tongue repeatedly. The Jacobson's organ in the roof of its mouth analyzes minute airborne particles from the forked tongue tips while also determining direction of the strongest or most desirable scent. Accumulated chemical cues help the snake zero in on potential prey while approaching within its preferred striking distance of less than 8 inches (20 cm).

An open-mouthed lunge attempts to sink the snake's teeth into the intended prey to anchor it while the snake's body whips forward and coils around it. The fore portion of the prey, especially the head or shoulder region, is often targeted in the strike. Presumably this allows better control of the struggling victim's mouth, which in the case of an adult rodent or bird may be a dangerous weapon capable of injuring the snake. The objective is then rapid immobilization. When all movement ceases, the grip is released so the corn snake can seek the prey's head where the swallowing process virtually always begins. The snake uses a combination of tactile cues from the overlap direction of the hair or feathers and rapid tongue flicks to find the best starting point. The gradually widening contour commencing at the narrow snout end of most prey animals, combined with the lay of the hair or feathers, lends itself to the slow engulfing process more readily than when swallowing food backwards. 'Breech feeding' is not unusual and rarely causes any difficulty unless the meal item is extremely large. It typically just takes a little longer, from a couple minutes to 20 minutes or more. All snakes are best left undisturbed during this feat when they feel vulnerable to attack and may spit out the food item if nervous.

Check Your Source
Domestically raised lab rodents address the nutritional needs of corn snakes admirably, largely due to the decades of exhaustive research behind formulation of the commercial laboratory chows used to conveniently feed and propagate most rodent colonies today. These large-pelleted diets are not necessarily used by all small-scale rodent breeders though; some opt for utilizing the cheapest dog foods and day-old bread that they can acquire to feed their mice and rats. Question your source of rodents thoroughly about the diet their stock is fed to better assess if your snakes' nutritional requirements will be met by using their animals.

RODENT BITES

Injuries resulting from bites by live rodents are a rare occurrence because corn snakes are very adept at subduing such prey *when they're hungry!* Problems happen most often when live adult rodents are left in a snake's cage for many hours, especially overnight. If the snake is dis-interested in feeding for any reason, incredibly it may allow a hungry or thirsty rodent to literally chew off its skin and flesh while lying in the cage seemingly unaware. The way to prevent this is quite simple – don't leave such potentially dangerous rodents in with your corns unat-tended. When you can't keep a constant eye on the situation inside the cage, at least leave some food like a slice of fruit and piece of bread or nut for the mouse or rat to nibble on. This reduces, but doesn't absolutely eliminate, all risk.

FROZEN RODENTS/COMMERCIAL SNAKE DIETS

Frozen rodents come in every size and description. They can be pur-chased at most pet shops that cater to herp-oriented clientele, or bought via mail-order quite easily today. Their greatest advantage is the convenience of having appropriately sized meals handily stashed away in your home freezer for whenever they're needed. Soaking the frozen prey in warm water, leaving them out at normal room tempera-tures on a tray, or even quick-thawing them in a microwave oven at the defrost setting (*not* full power or, *yecch, they explode!*), will prepare them for feeding to hungry corns. With the latter method, watch for hotspots on ends, or unthawed middles on bulky morsels. The freez-ing process breaks down food items' cell walls, inducing a stronger aroma to waft through the herp room as the food thaws which stimu-lates snakes' appetites. The same effect also makes thawed food more easily digested so that somewhat larger meals can be safely offered, and fully assimilated, by specimens not currently in the peak of health. Freezing of lizards, frogs, etc. that are sometimes used as food for juve-niles will also kill many pathogens and parasites that may be harbored inside. Most residential freezers do not reach cold enough tempera-tures to kill *all* bacteria, so re-freezing of uneaten food items is not rec-ommended.

This thawing preparation advice applies equally well to newly offered frozen *Snake Steak Sausages* by T-Rex™ Products, Chula Vista, California. They are made from whole ground vertebrate carcasses, including all parts except fur, feathers and intestines, cased in sausage skin units to take the place of actual rodents as herp food. The sausages are made in sizes ranging from those approximating a new-born mouse to a medium sized rat. They come in short connected chains resembling the old strings of hotdogs, making feeding multiple sections a cinch. A special *Mouse Maker* scenting fluid (*Lizard Maker* is also available) has even been devised to dab on the end of each to impart the smell of mice and complete the deception. The concept is old, but the actual product is new in the booming herp pet trade. *Snake Steak Sausages* may be a welcome answer for those objecting to frozen mice sharing home freezer space with the family steaks.

We tested two of the four manufactured sausage sizes at our home because we were particularly interested to see how juvenile *guttata* would respond. In a first-time test, a selected group of 47 voluntarily-feeding six-month-old corns were each offered one of the smallest

Mouse Maker-scented sausages. A single link was left in each snake's shoebox for one hour. On the initial try, 23 of them accepted the sausage with little hesitation, and 16 of the others took theirs during the following hour after we rubbed the rejected links with frozen mice. We were impressed with the fact that more than 75% of our young corns wolfed down the sausages on our first test evaluation.

Jon Coote in England reports that tests spanning five years on breeding colonies of colubrids, two-thirds of which were *Elaphe guttata*, yielded positive results raising babies to adulthood that were fed sausages for approximately 98% of their total dietary intake. Those same adults bred and produced healthy offspring, showing that the sausages appear capable of sustaining corns through their entire life cycle. An additional advantage is that the sausages don't tend to expand within snakes' stomachs like whole animals because the finely packed ground contents lack air pockets.

VITAMIN/MINERAL SUPPLEMENTS

An overwhelming number of vitamin and mineral supplements are available on the market today. They are largely intended to augment the more varied diets of omnivorous or strictly vegetarian herps that are difficult to duplicate in their broad spectrum. Even corn snakes benefit from extra nutrition found in the stomach contents, such as insects, seeds, and vegetation, of their usual prey. Captive corn diets may be deficient in an assortment of nutrients, so we see no harm in periodic supplementation of food items with any of the finely powdered products advertised in herp magazines - *as long as it's not done at every meal*. Although many of the vitamins are water-soluble, with excess amounts excreted quickly, and most don't easily build up to unnaturally toxic levels if only given sporadically, a few of the fat-soluble vitamins may accumulate. Adding calcium alone during breeding season may be especially valuable to females being bred intensively so that heavy egg production doesn't weaken them by drawing calcium from their skeletal systems.

Supplements are usually administered in one of several ways. The first is by dipping a food item into the product, which is either a fine powder or a liquid. Both types will stick to the prey animal. Dip only the rear end of a rodent because the strange new odor may confuse snakes if the head end that they normally seek first to ingest doesn't smell right. The liquid version may also be injected into pre-killed rodents with a syringe. A third strategy involves 'gut-loading' the feeder animals while they're alive, a technique that has been used for years on insects for lizards and amphibians. It could theoretically also be used on rodents by mixing special heavy doses of the supplement into a watery gruel of their normal chow, allowing it to dry into new enhanced food bricks, and giving it to hungry rodents just before using them as snake food. We'd suggest using rodents prepared in this way within a few hours before any of the products are passed and lost.

Meals distending a corn snake's profile any more than this are stressful and risk regurgitation if digestion conditions aren't perfect.

FEEDING METHODS

Offering dead food items of any kind is best done with forceps, large tweezers, or tongs to avoid bites by corns with excitable feeding responses. This is about the only time that they act like what could be deemed aggressive. Corns quickly learn to associate the opening of their cage and a hand entering as a signal to grab food before it escapes. Using a long, slender, less-noticeable instrument for offering food helps break the association between your hand and food so attempts to simply handle the snake are not always met with an open-mouthed charge. Another calming strategy is to first lift the snake out of its home cage with a snake hook and place it in a second empty container, such as a large plastic garbage can, to teach it that feeding always takes place in a separate feeding cage. This extra effort soon pays off when a corn is an unusually volatile feeder or if it's expected to be handled often, especially by children.

Use caution during feeding so excited corns don't strike wildly and injure themselves on instruments, cage walls, or furniture, or end up with mouths full of cage substrate if they miss the meal when they lunge. Their fervor doesn't always stop after the first food morsel either. We've often seen corns enter a sort of feeding frenzy immediately after the first item is barely down their gullets, quickly grabbing anything nearby that moves, or that is even bumped into. Be ready to take advantage of this behavior by having the next piece of food close at hand so it's what the snake sees first.

FEEDING STRATEGIES

Not every wild-caught corn will accept food in captivity, and even some captive-bred individuals balk at pre-killed food initially. Be prepared for several attempts at inducing them to eat voluntarily, using every trick at your disposal. First, try offering food just after dark when corns are normally beginning their daily hunting cycle. Try every possible combination of variably sized prey, live vs. dead, fresh killed vs. thawed frozen, and different kinds of prey. Various species of prey have distinctive smells and palatabilities to snakes, so try rats, hamsters, gerbils, day-old chicks, or any type of odd rodent you can find. Wild deer mice and white-footed mice of the genus *Peromyscus* are found throughout the natural range of *E. guttata* and are sometimes the key to getting a fussy corn's attention when all else fails. Introduce the food, only one item at a time, with minimal jarring of the cage so the snake isn't overly frightened by the intrusion. Leave it a few inches in front of the entrance hole to the snake's hiding place. *Do not* touch the snake's body or nose with the food – this will only scare a nervous captive. Get out of the room so peace and quiet reign, and don't come back for at least ten minutes so the shyest snake can eat undisturbed. Don't turn the light on when you do return to check; use a small flashlight to view the cage.

Next in our arsenal of methods is offering food from tweezers, forceps, tongs, etc. These tools' slender profiles don't scare snakes like a thick arm and hand in front of their snouts. We've found the 18-inch (46 cm) scissors-style stainless steel hemostat forceps the handiest to maneuver. 'Mechanical fingers' devices sold at auto parts stores also work well. With a dead rodent held at the tip, approach the snake from a low angle (high angle approaches may spook the snake) to let it see and smell the item. Keep very still so as not to distract it with any motions from your own body – you want its total attention riveted to the object in front of it. Slowly wave it around the vicinity of the corn's head, at the same time studying the snake's reaction. The trick is not to be intimidating, but instead to tempt it to strike a small helpless item that appears unthreatening. If the snake advances toward the item, back the prey away to gently induce the snake to give chase. Move the food further away and to the side to draw the snake out of its lair until it feels confident enough to attack. When it does, cease all movement – don't even breathe – while it constricts the prey and hopefully follows through and eats the food.

New on the market are "Snake Steak Sausages" – little links of ground whole animals made in several sizes that provide the closest thing to replacing a diet of rodents. They can be conveniently kept frozen until thawed when needed.

If the snake is out of its shelter, you can sometimes stimulate interest in the prey item by gently touching or stroking the snake's midbody with the rodent held in the forceps. Avoid direct contact with the snake's head because it interprets this as a frontal attack, causing it to respond in fear or anger. You want instead to elicit curiosity and a feeding strike. Again try the teasing action of trying to get the snake to follow the rodent after it turns to face the prey, pausing when it seems ready to pounce. Keep the rodent's nose low and pointing forward at all times so the prey will slide into the snake's mouth easily when bitten. Be slow and patient, and be ready to freeze once the bait is taken. Be alert in noting a snake's responses to your varied movements so you can refine your method through trial and error.

There may be times when you wish to push a corn for maximum growth, or build it up quickly after sickness or laying a huge clutch of eggs. If your time or patience is at a minimum, use the simple "dump 'em and run" method of just placing the additional prey item(s) on a piece of paper or plastic in the cage. This will make them available as second or third meals that many snakes will eagerly seek and devour after finishing the first. A piece of newspaper left underneath the food helps minimize the amount of substrate material that clings and is accidentally ingested. Such debris usually passes through corns' digestive tracts without incident, but it can cause impactions in the gut, especially if small snakes swallow large or sharp pieces.

Corns seem to only stay interested in eating for about 15 minutes per instance of feeding. If no new opportunities come along within that amount of time after the initial item is consumed, they usually lose interest and settle back into their favorite retreat, showing no further desire to eat. With a greater investment of time and effort, you can use a technique called "chain-feeding" to increase the size of each meal. Carefully ease a second food item between the snake's jaws as it's finishing the first. It will often continue engulfing the extra-long meal without noticing the deception if you place the prey in with a gentle touch. This methodology is rarely necessary with hardy corn snakes, but it's quite handy for giving medicines or other supplements stuffed inside a second meal that you want to be certain is ingested. Sometimes such materials exude a disagreeable odor that snakes will avoid if left to examine at their leisure.

We always try to avoid touching food items any more than is necessary so their natural smell is not removed or masked by our own. This is particularly important when handling pinkies, which do not possess the powerful attractant scent of larger rodents. We keep pinkies and fuzzies in a tray with aromatic bin bedding from the adults' cages until they're fed to the snakes. It also acts as an enticing announcement that the opportunity to feed is near if you leave the pans of food items in your snake area for 15 minutes in advance. The "dinner fragrance" will waft across the room and heighten your corns' anticipation levels.

COAXING STUBBORN
HATCHLINGS TO FEED

Most hatchling corn snakes being produced for today's market recognize pinkie mice as food. Keep in mind that lizards and frogs are also normal, if not preferred, starter food items of hatchling corns in the wild. The emphasis we've put on getting them to recognize and eat baby mice is based upon convenience for keepers. There's nothing wrong with offering them their natural foods, if those kinds of items are available to you, at the beginning of their lives to start them off with less stress. Freezing those cold-blooded animals prior to using them will largely eliminate the threat of parasite transfer.

Corns' willingness to accept mice from the start is undoubtedly at least partially responsible for their immense popularity as pets. It's also certainly no coincidence. As herpetoculturists established the numerous color and pattern morphs we have today, they also selectively bred against, through attrition, those that were difficult to raise. This helped eliminate those possessing a disinclination to feed on baby mice from passing their genes along to further generations. As a result, we'd estimate that less than 5% of neonate corns would be included in the stubborn starter category today, and this percentage should continue to decline. Certain bloodlines or morphs tend to have higher ratios of difficult pinkie mouse feeders, though many outgrow their obstinacy following several meals passing through and "kick-starting" their digestive systems.

For that inevitable annoying holdout that somehow ends up in your collection anyway, a number of tricks may help you persuade it to accept baby mice for you. The first is to be sure that it's housed alone in a comfortable cage environment as described earlier, one that's not so large that the food gets lost in the wide open spaces and is never found by the snake. Be sure it has found the water too and is well hydrated before attempting to feed it. The temperature should be in the mid-80s°F (28-31°C) with high humidity. A light misting of the cage with lukewarm water may be of additional value in stimulating appetite. Keeping their crepuscular (active at dusk) nature in mind, gently introduce the tiniest live pinkie you can obtain into the cage just in front of the entrance to the hidebox around sunset. Quickly vacate the room to avoid spooking the shy snakeling, and do not return to check progress until at least the next morning.

If the first effort fails, repeat the process the following evening, but this time place the snake and pinkie together into a four-inch (10 cm) diameter empty deli cup with a few ventilation holes and an opaque lid for privacy. The idea is to give the snake just one thing to concentrate upon all night, and it works about 50% of the time. If necessary, the procedure can be tried a third time with a freshly killed pinkie. Occasionally an active pinkie frightens a shy snake too much, so the motionless food item is more enticing. "Braining" a prekilled mouse by skinning the head exposes the stronger scent of bodily fluids that tempt some snakes into action. Thawed mice may also have the same increased olfactory arousal effect. Try the deli cup method at least three times before moving on to more drastic procedures.

When none of this works, it's time to resort to disguise-scenting the mouse's body with the aroma of a different prey species that may trigger an instinctual feeding response. Find an anole, swift, gecko, or other small lizard species that many corns eat in the wild as their first

Tease-feeding a stubborn baby corn first involves gently restraining it in one hand while offering a baby mouse to it with the other. You want the snake to forget the fact that it's being held in your hand.

Hold the pinkie inches away from its snout, bumping it against the snake's body – not its head! – until the corn lunges for it. Cease all motion when the snake connects by sinking its teeth into the mouse.

Don't move a muscle as the snake decides whether to continue swallowing or releasing the morsel in its mouth. Let the snake finish swallowing the meal before laying it down.

meals. Use it to thoroughly impregnate the pinkie by rubbing the mouse against the lizard's moistened skin. As before, body fluids have greater appeal, so breaking the lizard's tail and smearing blood onto the mouse creates a stronger attractant. A partially skinned frozen lizard can also do the job and be saved in a resealable plastic bag and reused many times if necessary. If one kind of lizard fails to tempt, try others until you find one that pleases the finicky feeder's palate. Some breeders advocate washing baby rodents in warm water prior to any artificial scenting to further eliminate any natural rodent odor that the snake may find distracting.

The next tool in your arsenal is tease-feeding. Fortunately, corns are fairly easy to induce to feed via this method if you can muster the necessary patience. Hold the snake firmly but gently with one hand around its mid-section, enclosing its body with a closed four-fingered fist and leaving its tail hanging out below. Only two or three inches of the corn's head and neck should be sticking up free above your curled index finger. With the other hand, hold a small pre-killed pinkie mouse with the head protruding out past your fingertips, and use it to gently "beat" the snake along the *posterior* third of its body. Avoid touching the snake's head and upper body as this only induces a fright response. The idea is to tease it enough to make the snake strike out in anger or curiosity at the object pestering its flank, but not send it cringing in fear of its head being 'attacked.' What you hope will happen is that the snake lunges out, grabs the pinkie, *and hangs on!* If it doesn't, try, try again until it finally latches on and decides to "keep" it. Let go and unobtrusively remove your other hand from sight.

Now comes the patience part! You must remain dead still – *Ignore that fly on your nose!* - and let the baby snake forget about everything except the object in its mouth. It will usually spend from a few seconds to a minute or two "contemplating" the morsel, and then, if you've succeeded in not spooking it, start to swallow. Any distraction at this point may cause it to withdraw and drop the mouse, at which point the next attempt may be even tougher. Remain completely motionless until the lump disappears down the throat and out of sight. Then gently put the snake back in its cage and don't disturb it for a couple days – *you* and it need the rest! The good news is that baby corns are usually quick to accept food this way, making it a relatively painless process after only two or three sessions. We've found having the TV on while engaged in doing this initially tedious task helps the time pass more quickly.

FORCE-FEEDING

Force-feeding is the last desperation step in dealing with a non-feeder, and should only be attempted when all the above steps at voluntary feeding fail. Don't resort to this method too soon though because otherwise healthy neonates can easily go four weeks without eating as long as fresh drinking water is present. The routine is potentially dangerous for a fragile little snake and is stressful on snake and owner alike. Hold the snake as when tease-feeding, but this time leave only its head free. Have a thin metal or plastic rod, such as a slender side of the knitting needle, handy. If the snake refuses to open its mouth, use the rod to carefully pry it open, trying not to damage any teeth. Insert the nose of the tiniest available pinkie, a severed pinkie head, or a severed mouse tail, as deeply as possible, keeping a slight pressure on the rear end of the prey so it's not immediately expelled. A little water or butter will help lubricate the prey so it slides down more easily. Use a round-tipped rod to carefully prod it down into the gullet until it disappears from sight, and then gently massage the food down from the outside for at least a couple more inches. Once there, it'll probably either come back out within a matter of minutes, or settle down further into the stomach and be digested normally.

Food can also be forced into a snake's belly using a plastic hypodermic syringe with a thin flexible tube, such as a human catheter, affixed to the end in place of a needle. For tiny hatchlings, special three to four inch (8-10 cm) stainless steel feeding tubes, obtained from veterinary suppliers, may be attached to 10-20 cc syringes for the same purpose. Finely ground cat food, or strained meat baby food makes suitable mixtures for a couple of fast meals to stimulate a snake's appetite. They may not be completely balanced diets for snakes though and should be thought of only as emergency measures. A 1 cc quantity of the formula is enough for one feeding to a baby corn that is 12 inches (30 cm) long.

The "Pinkie Pump," made by BJ Specialties, Boerne, Texas, is a custom-made stainless steel syringe that purées and pushes whole dead pinkies down a snake's throat via a short hollow tube built into the end, all in one action. Its basic advantage is that it delivers whole food, which is a better diet overall than the fill-in measures above. It's still not intended to be more than a temporary measure while getting a problem snake "back on its feet."

If a baby snake does not start eating voluntarily within a few months, it will probably never be a healthy specimen. A very low percentage of hatchlings, after your best efforts, will persist in their determination to slowly starve to death. At that point, you may have to accept that it just wasn't in the cards for them to survive. Mother Nature intended for them to be food for other wildlife, and nothing you could do would change it. Consider euthanizing a weak specimen by freezing, accepting the loss, and moving on to concentrate on the other healthy animals that need your attention. If you persist and manage to raise a severe problem feeder to adulthood and breed it, you may expect that the genes governing its finicky feeding behavior may also be passed, compounding the hassle many fold in future generations.

GROWTH AND LONGEVITY

The corns in today's market are descended from stock collected from all over their natural range. Certain populations tend to consist of smaller individuals, adults at a mere 30 inches (76 cm), such as some in the lower peninsula of Florida and the Keys. Others from the lower mid-Atlantic states regularly grow to a husky 5-6 feet (1.5–1.8 m). Egg clutch size and hatchling length are also influenced by the locality and genetics of their ancestors. Corns from northeastern Florida frequently lay 30 or more smallish eggs per clutch, the hatchlings of which may be a petite 9-10 inches (23–25 cm). Contrast those with the 13+ inch (33+ cm) neonates that can come from a clutch of only eight to 12 huge eggs of an *E. g. emoryi* from Oklahoma. Knowing your snakes' ancestral origins may help you plan for these characteristics when choosing breeding stock.

Baby corns that are growing rapidly can convert up to a third of the weight of food into added body mass, and they can double their lengths easily the first year. In fact, with an above-average devotion of time and feeding effort on your part, corns may achieve the minimal breeding size of about 30 inches (76 cm) at nine to ten months of age. Most keepers, however, raise their corns to sexual maturity in about 18–20 months, at which time they are typically in the 36–42 inch (91–107 cm) range. Wild corns typically mature in their second or third year of growth at 3-3 ½ feet (91-107 cm) for females and 3 ½-5 feet (107-152 cm) for males on a normal feeding regimen. Corns may shed their skins up to eight times during their first year when food is abundant. The rate slows to two to four times per year after adulthood is reached.

Adulthood is positively a factor of size, not age, in *Elaphe guttata*. The youngest successfully bred female has been reliably recorded as being 27 inches (68 cm) in total length and a mere eight months of age. In this accidental mating with a sibling brother, two of the five eggs laid hatched. It's prudent to note that this is an extreme which should be left to the record books, not become normal husbandry practice. Reproduction by females much under three feet (.9 m) in length and less than about three-quarters of a pound (0.34 kg) in weight is a strain due to the significant weight loss and dehydration affecting their barely mature bodies. Besides a tendency to lay only a few large eggs, their susceptibility to egg-binding and other reproductive problems is higher than normal too.

Males have fewer health concerns than females at the beginning of their reproductive lives; it's mostly a matter of whether they will or won't breed, period! We've noticed that young males are often sexually naïve during their first encounter with females, crawling around them while not quite knowing exactly what to do next in a discernible show of "curious clumsiness." We've seen no harm in trying them early, and have noted that they virtually always figure things out within a couple weeks when their next chance to breed occurs.

Males grow longer and heavier than females. The biggest brutes top out at 6 feet (183 cm) and about 2 pounds (nearly 1 kg) in weight. Most corns over

4 ½ feet (137 cm) are in fact males, and corns over 5 feet (1.5 m) are seldom seen in captivity. This may be a consequence of the vast amount of inbreeding involved in modern propagation efforts. Pairing those occasional huge males with tiny females, or vice versa, has never been an insurmountable obstacle to corns mating in our experience, except for the slight worry about one physically crushing the other in an unusually cramped cage. Growth and shedding frequency steadily slows down after maturity, although it seems to continue almost imperceptibly for the duration of life.

LONGEVITY

The documented longevity record in captivity for any specimen of *Elaphe guttata* stands at 32 years and 3 months. Records for zoo display animals have easily surpassed two decades in several instances. Corns that live peaceful lives with little stress are more capable of achieving such lifespans. This is especially true of individuals that are not part of breeding colonies whose aim is to produce mega numbers of neonates, including the physically taxing expectation of double-clutching. Without precise figures to back these claims, the experience of all our colleagues confirms that intensive breeding causes corn snakes to age prematurely. At the time of writing, we personally have a few specimens in the 13-14 year old range that are still successfully reproducing. Mark Hazel reports that he has a 16-year-old female corn that's still quite prolific and 'going strong', laying and hatching 19 eggs this year. That snake has been reproducing since it was only two years of age. Yet at 10–12 years of age, we've also seen specimens with geriatric symptoms such as general loss of musculature, ridged backbones protruding on specimens otherwise in good weight, chronically gaping mouths, permanently cloudy eyes, and general reproductive failure "for no apparent reason." We know others have undoubtedly surpassed these stated upper limits, and will probably continue to do so as herpetological nutrition and husbandry techniques improve in the future.

INTELLIGENCE

Instinct seems to play a vastly greater role in snakes' survival than learning. Still, corns obviously possess a certain ability to remember their surroundings because they excel at returning faithfully to favorite shelters and finding water sources in the wild and in captivity. They're known to reutilize avenues of escape from cages again in a fraction of the time it took them to discover them the first time. They also definitely learn from negative experiences such as after being nipped by the first weaned rat they tackle after a former diet of mice, whereby they often refuse rats as prey of any size from then onward.

And then, we've witnessed the frequent claims by hobbyists that their pets 'know and trust' them by exhibiting calmer actions in their presence or while in their grasp. We know how anthropomorphic people tend to get at times, but we try to keep an open mind to the chance that there's more here than simple chemosensory recognition. We're particularly keen to hear about additional phenomena of apparent intelligence in corn snakes, especially if they include any kind of experimental method or other evidence beyond mere feelings.

SHEDDING (ECDYSIS)

Snakes periodically shed (slough) their skins, replacing the old, less flexible outer layer with a newer, cleaner, and more elastic layer of skin as they grow. They also shed sooner and more often in response to skin injuries, speeding up the healing process over that given time period. The part of this process that we can witness on the snake externally takes about seven to ten days from start to finish. One day the colors suddenly appear much duller than usual. Within a day or two, the snake's eyes cloud over with a milky or bluish cast. This condition persists for several more days, and then disappears for an additional several days prior to the actual molting. Snakes become more shy and reclusive than usual during this period, and their usual calm attitude may temporarily be replaced by nervousness, or readiness to nip your hand. Their appetites wane, too, but reappear with a vengeance as soon as the old skins are discarded.

When it's time to shed, a corn will actively explore its cage, constantly rubbing its snout against walls, substrate, and any cage furniture encountered in an attempt to loosen the old skin from its nose and chin. Once started, it crawls forward to work the skin off, like peeling a tight stocking off your foot. If all goes well, the skin rolls off inside out in one continuous piece, with the tail of the shed pointing in the direction the snake traveled. This might be handy to

A corn snake in the blue-eyed or opaque state will be shedding its skin in approximately four to seven days. Note the dull lackluster appearance of its colors during this period.

know when a recently cast skin is discovered in the field and you're wondering which way the former occupant went.

A freshly shed skin is pliable, feels moist to the touch, and should even contain the clear spectacles that covered the eyes and every scale down to the tail tip. Too low humidity and/or poor diet can cause the skin to peel off in pieces, leaving scattered areas where it sticks fast. If patches of dry skin remain on the body, they should be removed manually to avoid bacteria gaining a foothold growing under the layers. First try the easy route of leaving the snake overnight in a sack full of wet crumpled newspapers or rags so it can crawl through them and possibly loosen the old skin by itself. If this fails, soak the snake in water for at least 15 minutes to soften the problem areas. Then sandwich the snake between some rough towels, and let it force its way through, which usually pulls the problem areas free. Be sure to notice that every inch of old skin is removed right down to the tail tip. That's where an accumulation of stuck, dry skins can restrict blood flow and eventually kill the tail tissue, causing it to slough off, leaving a slight stubbed tip.

If either eyecap does not appear intact in the sloughed head portion of the skin, it may create a place for an infection to start. For this reason, most keepers opt to remove eyecaps manually. First try rubbing your thumb over the eye in an attempt to partially dislodge an edge of the stuck cap. We've found that tweezers with pointy tips are the handiest tool to get a hold of the extra skin covering stuck at the edge of the eye. Use a wet sponge to swab the eyes first to soften them a little, but avoid the use of glycerin or any other skin softening product intended for humans. Gently fish around for a solid grip on the edge of the eyecap, slide a tip under it, and simply lift it away. This sounds difficult and may make you squeamish, but the tough spectacles of serpents' eyes are not nearly as sensitive to slight bumping or as easily injured as those of humans. On the other hand, extreme caution must be taken to be sure that only the extra cap is grasped with the tweezers, and not the cornea itself.

A word of reassurance - don't fret if you're not ready to tackle this kind of operation. We've rarely seen a single stuck eyecap actually develop into a serious problem. The easiest, safest route is to just wait for the caps to come off with the next molt, which they nearly always do. You can facilitate that likelihood by leaving a plastic storage tub, half full of damp moss or paper towels, in the cage when the snake's eyes next cloud over prior to shedding. The snake will then have the choice of preparing in advance for the next shed by pre-loosening its eyecaps and skin in a moist cozy retreat.

PART II BREEDING

As fascinating as corn snakes are to keep and enjoy, inducing them to reproduce in captivity takes it all to the next level. Successful procreation is the ultimate proof that your care of their needs has been adequate for them to fulfill the most important function of their lives. And, it's interesting, educational, and maybe even profitable to propagate corn snakes as an adjunct to your hobby. This chapter will be handled as one long chronological dialogue to best illustrate the subject in detail.

SEXING SNAKES

Knowing the sex of corns is an essential first step in efforts to breed them. It can be determined with varying degrees of accuracy in many different ways, the most basic of which is simply putting them together and observing which ones actually mate. This will demonstrate the sexes with 100% certainty, but doesn't allow any future planning of pairings. Besides, most corns are acquired as juveniles one or more years ahead of the time they will hopefully be used in reproduction, so judging the sex of them in advance is a necessity. A successful breeder must personally master one or more methods of sexing snakes to break

It's not hard to judge the sex of adult corns by the relative proportions of the base of their tails. Here we have alternating tails of males and females, starting with a male on top. Males' tails run thicker for the first couple inches just past the vent, whereas females' tail-bases taper quickly, starting right past that point.

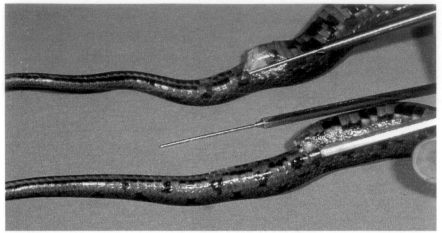

Probing corn snakes. In a female (top), the sexing probe will barely enter the tail area. In a male (bottom), it will penetrate to a depth at least equal to four times the width of the tail.

dependence on others' ability or honesty for that vital information. Mistakes in sexing run rampant in the pet industry and have spoiled many projects when mis-sexed specimens are only discovered after years of raising them to breeding age. Much more often than not, the error turns out to be that a presumed female is actually a male.

Male snakes have an intricate bilobed sex organ called the hemipenes; each one of

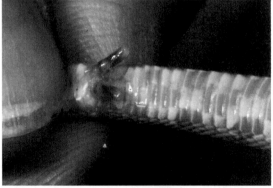

With a little practice, the hemipenes of baby corns can be manually everted by gentle pressure applied by the thumb from the tail forward towards the vent. They usually appear pink or red, but may also look pale whitish or nearly clear.

the two prongs of it is called a hemipenis. These lie inside-out in the base of their tails starting at the cloacal (combined copulatory and defecation) opening. Popping out and thus exposing the hemipenes of baby or small juvenile snakes is fast and easy once you've mastered the knack of it; it's not as easily done once corns exceed about 18 inches (46 cm) in total length. With the belly of the snakeling facing up, hold the tail between your thumb and index finger, with the tip of your thumb about ½ to 3/4 inch (1–1.5 cm) behind the cloacal (vent) opening. Apply light downward pressure with the thumb tip while also pushing forward toward the vent. *If* it's a male, this will evert one or both hemipenises and force them to emerge from the vent as they would when used in mating. They may look like clear, white, pink, or red protuberances about 3/16 to 1/4 inch (5-7 mm) long and as slender as toothpicks. If done gently, the practice is harmless to corn snakes, and the organs will slip back inside and disappear from sight as soon as the pressure is released. Female snakes have no such extrudable appendages in their tails, although snakes of both sexes have small scent glands that occasionally

Corns mate with their tails raised and joined at the vents. The male (below) everts one hemipenis into the female's slightly gaping cloaca in a split-second pulse after she raises her tail as an "invitation".

"peek" out at the edges of the cloaca, never more than 1/16 inch (1 mm), to fool inexperienced keepers.

Another less dependable method, similar to candling eggs for signs of fertility, uses a strong, narrow-beamed light aimed up through a baby *amelanistic* corn's body from the dorsal side of the tail base region while viewing this area from the belly side. In many cases, the hemipenes will show up as elongated darkened spots on each side of the centerline of the tail just behind the cloaca. The lack of black skin pigment of amelanistic corns allows them to show up through the surrounding clear or white ventral scutes. This organ is not always obvious, but can usually be discerned with some practice involving many specimens for comparison.

Probing is the standard method employed by specialists to sex snakes of any size or age. This method uses slender metal or plastic rods with rounded tips called sexing probes and obtainable from businesses that sell reptile supplies. To probe a snake, the round tip of the probe is inserted very carefully in one of two tiny openings at the base of the tail, visible when one gently pulls up the anal plate to expose the cloacal opening. In males the tiny openings enter the inverted hemipenises. In females they lead to post-anal glands. The probe's diameter should be only 1/32 inch (<1 mm) for neonates, or up to 1/16 inch (<2 mm) for specimens over a yard (meter) in length. It is moistened with water or a non-oil-based lubricant like K-Y Jelly™ first, then poked around under the vent plate in the direction of the tail and slightly off-center until it slips into one of the resting hemipenises. This is done with only the lightest pressure behind the action so as not to forcibly puncture the organ and penetrate the muscular tissue beyond it. The probe, upon reaching the end of a male organ, has a slightly bouncy or springy feel to it; hitting the back of the small pocket of a female's scent gland feels

The skin of this gravid female is clearly stretched over the obviously heavy rear one-third of her swollen body that's packed with eggs ready to be laid.

more like a dull thud against something relatively solid. Hemipenises are only about 3/8 inch (1 cm) deep in new hatchlings, but up to about 3 inches (77 mm) in large adult males. If the probe enters to that depth on either side without being pushed too hard, you're relatively assured of having a male. A probe will barely enter a female's tail for more than the distance equal to the width of the tail at the vent of any size corn snake.

Clear or translucent food storage containers make great nesting chambers for corns. Fill them two-thirds full of moist sphagnum moss or other medium to provide a suitable place for the female to deposit her clutch of eggs.

The last and simplest way to deduce the sex of an adult corn is to visually gauge the shape of its tail, especially the base region. Males have longer tails that run the same width for the next two to three inches (5-7.5 cm) past the cloaca. Females' tails taper abruptly just after the vent, mainly because they don't house the space-consumptive sex organs of the males. The sexes are a cinch to notice and differentiate after studying and learning to recognize the subtle nuances in tail shape. The skill needed is innate in all of us, related to the ability you have to instantly discern the slightest profile variations of human members of the opposite sex, even from great distances. This method is virtually 100% accurate by someone experienced at judging many snakes, but should generally be backed-up by probing when any doubt exists.

PREBREEDING CONDITIONING

Corn snakes follow a fairly typical reptilian reproductive cycle, with mating in spring and egg laying during late spring to early summer. The eggs hatch over the summer, and all snakes go through a variably strict dormant period during the cooler months. Environmental stimuli control the timing of these events annually. Allowing your corns to experience such seasonal changes keeps their internal biological clocks ticking on schedule so these natural events bring about successful breeding in captivity. The difference between summer's warmth and winter's lower temperatures are so blatantly obvious that many herpetoculturists use manipulation of temperature alone to induce their herps to breed. It often works, and some species apparently reproduce well without a change in photoperiod! In our opinion, temperature and photoperiod are both important triggers of reproduction in corns. Facilitating each influence's impact on successful breeding can be incredibly simple to accomplish since each is easy to control in your home. This chapter will help you avoid repeating the fundamental errors of basic herp keeping of only a half century ago, when essentially healthy snakes were maintained, but they *hardly ever reproduced!*

The vast majority of keepers maintain their collections indoors, so synchronizing reproduction depends on making their snakes aware of the progression of seasons. This can be done through artificial means anywhere in a home where a cool area can be maintained for two to three months of the year. If the situation also allows natural light to be the main source of daily light for the cages, by putting them near an outside window or skylight, so much the better! If the exposure is sufficiently large, the sun may also affect the room (or cage) temperature to reflect the gradually changing trend outdoors. This necessarily links your corns' breeding cycle to your latitude, but is a tried and true method for positive results.

If your animal-keeping area happens to be in a cool, dark basement in a northern climate, artificial heaters and lights on electric timers can replicate the increasing or decreasing temperatures and day lengths of the seasons. Totally controlling these environmental cues may be expensive but has the advantage of allowing earlier or later breeding and hatching to suit owners' time schedules or to coincide with better marketing periods.

To better explain replicating a typical reproductive cycle for corn snakes by example, let's assume a starting point for our breeding plans in the autumn, after the main summer active season is over, and follow the typical routine we use in southern Florida. We'll ignore the previous breeding season and note only that our snakes have been feeding well all summer and early fall, look fat and healthy, and are either already adults or will likely reach adult proportions within months and be ready for next year. This does not apply to thin or otherwise health-compromised specimens, which are best kept separately in a warm, well-lit place where they will continue to feed and recover. It is also unnecessary to subject juvenile corns to reproductive cycling during their first year of life. You may safely skip this conditioning phase and simply grow them up a little faster with no harm done during their initial winter season.

Look ahead at your schedule over the coming months and choose a date for the start of your snakes' winter dormancy period. We often designate mid December as our target date to let the room temperature drop. This, *not* coincidentally, is just before Christmas, and is also (significantly) about the shortest day of the year in the northern hemisphere. At least two weeks prior to that date, all feeding should come to a complete halt. For those couple weeks until mid December, we maintain the warm temperatures our corns have enjoyed for the last few months to allow enough time for all food to pass through their digestive tracts. We don't want undigested food, or even old fecal matter, resting in the snakes' guts during dormancy to invite contamination. Fresh water is kept available at all times, regardless of all other parameters.

During this time, the windows and skylights are blocked to severely cut the natural outside light intensity. Some people merely draw the blinds or curtains to block off most of the light, which might simulate winter conditions during the cooler months when the sun is less intense and above the horizon for fewer hours. Others advise cutting off all ambient light to super-stimulate snakes into "thinking" it's the dead of winter, as in a subterranean hibernaculum in southern New Jersey. Corns span such latitudes in nature and are adapted to handle both extremes, so you may wish to experiment with the intensity of winter your colony is subjected to, trying a milder version at first.

Reduced daily photoperiod in winter stimulates certain hormonal processes months ahead of actual reproduction for many plant and animal species. Farmers have long known that manipulating the photoperiod can control everything from when flowers bloom to getting more and larger eggs from poultry. Common sense dictates that light cycles affect reptilian breeding cycles too, yet few people think about light beyond whether their herps need ultraviolet wavelengths to bask under or not. It's even easier to control than heat, so we can't imagine approaching herpetoculture without planning to use photoperiod to our advantage along with controlling temperature.

After the digestive tract flushing out period, the heat is shut off, or at least cut back considerably. The idea here is to let corns experience a cooler period than that in which they're active for the rest of the year. This coincides naturally with the shorter day lengths of winter. Decades of experience have taught us that this period does not have to be very exact or constant, just noticeably lower so the snakes' reproductive systems know "it's that time." Spermatogenesis and ovarian follicle development, the internal formation of male and female sex cells, need this cooler rest period. The exact limits of when it starts or ends, or how long it takes, remain debatable. Due to yearly fluctuations in the weather, it's safe to say that no precise formula exists to trigger them, nor must one be strictly adhered to in captivity for successful results.

We aim for a cool season in the 45-65°F (7–18°C) range for about 60–75 days, but it's not a factor that must be critically monitored or controlled. Corns can handle "hibernation" periods of three months easily and safely; some herpetoculturists recommend a longer rest, for both the snakes and themselves. Our room regularly rises into the upper 70s°F (24-27°C), and even into the mid 80s°F (29-30°C) during occasional afternoons on the coldest months of January-February with no perceivable ill effects on our colony. When that happens, after all, it's even warmer outside where native corns live and breed in the woods near our home. Conversely, the thermometer also dips into the upper 30s°F (3-4°C) on a few nights most winters, with no detrimental effects from such lows either. We've learned not to fret the odd extremes. As long as they don't persist for more than a day or two at a time, and it stays generally cooler for the majority of the dormancy period, that's apparently sufficient. Corns' natural range spans 15 degrees of latitude; they are equipped to handle temperature extremes of short duration. We recommend individual experimentation with the intensity of winter your colony is subjected to based on these broad guidelines.

Occasionally, winters bathe South Florida in unseasonably mild temperatures for stretches of many weeks. One of those ideal tourist winters in the late 1990s was freakishly warm, sparing us from a freeze at all. Severe exceptions like that may adversely affect reproduction because we noticed somewhat lower fertility in eggs the following spring-summer season. We could attribute it to no other reason. To combat such phenomena, we've resorted to air conditioning the room during excessive heatwaves to try to keep it below 65°F (18°C) over those spells. A hibernation period consistently above this level can cause snakes to burn fat reserves and enter the spring reproductive season thinner and weaker than they should be.

We barely disturb our corns during the entire 2-2½ month cool period, as would be the case in the field if they were inactive underground or in tree cavities. Replacing their drinking water and bowl once per week is the only reason we bother them during that time. Toward mid-February, we uncover the windows. A week or so later, we turn on the heat, especially at night, to send a strong message that spring has begun. The salient point we hope to convince the snakes' reproductive systems of is that there's no turning back once the light levels increase and the land begins to warm up. We don't want to allow a late cold snap to disrupt the orderly procession of hormonally-influenced reproductive events in our snakes' bodies.

If you live in a latitude that permits you to maintain your specimens outdoors most or all of the year, or in a room well lit with bright skylights, nature will largely take care of temperature and lighting for you. The miniscule lengthening of each consecutive day in spring, combined with the steadily increasing warmth that accompanies it, will be sensed directly by all corns living under semi-natural conditions. If your situation calls for depending heavily upon artificial fluorescent lighting to simulate this spring intensification, it's important to note that most bulbs' output is tiny compared to the sun. Counter by using lots of bulbs, and place them as close as possible to your animals to enhance their effect.

In addition, set the 'on' duration to increase by approximately one half hour per week once you've begun the warm-up period, and continue doing this over the next several months. This reverses the trend of winter, which subjects them to more hours of darkness than light, by increasing the daily photoperiod by six hours over three months' time until the days are longer than the nights again. This is another way of super-stimulating them to know that "spring has sprung." Many organisms have a distinct threshold of intuitively knowing the level of daylight hours per day, and/or the intensity of light that must be surpassed to induce certain biochemical reactions. It seems that neither aspect is absolutely necessary for corns to breed successfully. Still, our instincts tell us that it's part of nature's overall recipe, and that exposing them to the parameters described above is beneficial.

All this effort of simulating spring's arrival to your entire collection at the same time is to assure that corn snake hormones will flow in unison. You want your males' and females' reproductive physiologies to be primed to procreate at the same time. Then when they finally have access to each other during the period when the females are "in heat," both sexes will be ready and instinctively know how to proceed.

Following a few days of warm, digestion-friendly temperatures, a single, smaller-than-normal rodent is offered. We start snakes on an easily handled meal to assure that their digestive systems are functioning smoothly after the "big sleep." The next meal follows in a week or less and is back to the size and weight that is typical for each individual corn snake. From then on, they're fed to their stomachs' content for several weeks so they put on weight rapidly. This is not to replace grams lost during winter, as healthy specimens hardly lose any weight. Our real goal is for the females to acquire extra bulk in preparation for producing eggs soon. Obligingly, they seem to add weight unusually quickly at this time. Many older juveniles also seem to bulk up and suddenly acquire adult proportions during the spring feeding frenzy, presumably in a biologically-governed rush to be available in case the opportunity arises to pass on their genes *this* season. Ovulation, the production of egg masses in the elongated ovaries, typically starts five to eight weeks after the spring warm-up and post-hibernation feeding commences.

BREEDING

How do we know when to start breeding our corn snakes in spring? How can we tell when each one is ready? We concentrate almost entirely on our females' physical conditions. Post-hibernation shedding, often several weeks and many meals after the warm-up time started, is generally believed to be a reliable signal of the start of the active breeding season. Females may mate successfully then, prior to ovulation, by holding the sperm in waiting until their own egg follicles are mature in a few more weeks. We've noted that matings during this early period typically take longer to be initiated because the females seem less eager to breed then, compared to the period after ovulation.

Experience helps in recognizing the subtle signs of actual ovulation in females - mainly the bulging rear halves of their bodies. A moderately stiff swelling may be noticeable in the lower center of their lengths too when it first begins. After we've been feeding females steadily for about a month, we start noticing which ones are bulking up earliest and we begin mentally quantifying the degree of skin showing between their scales. Their appearance very much resembles the well-fed look of snakes with recently digested food spread out in their guts, with a couple of slight differences. The bulges tend to be more lateral and soft and squishy to the touch. The belly's ventral scutes take on a more curved appearance, as opposed to the squared-off, flat-bottomed look of non-ovulating specimens.

We've perfected a simple little trick to check for ovulating females by feel: Rest your hand on a tabletop, laying a soft sheer cloth or handkerchief on your upward-facing palm, and keeping your fingers slightly spread. Let the female in question slowly crawl across your four fingers in a direction perpendicular to them. If she's ovulating, the subtle sensation should remind you vaguely of a string of pearls, bumping along over each finger's hump as it passes. When you get good at it, you can use the same technique to estimate how many eggs there will be or to count the eggs once they are fertilized inside her.

Don't worry about the males' willingness to cooperate in breeding. Unless they're about to shed (and sometimes even then), when a female is ready to mate, they'll be ready too! Males are sometimes agitated at this time and may occasionally bite stray hands. It's also significant to note that some male corns may only feed sporadically, or not at all, during the breeding season as their sexual appetites seemingly override their need for caloric nourishment. They'll normally resume feeding after mating season has passed. If not, it helps to remove them from the vicinity of the females to limit exposure to the "come get me" pheromone barrage in the air that may still be distracting them. Certain males consistently begin breeding earlier in the season than other males, and some retain interest later into the summer too.

If you don't trust your judgement, you can always revert to the old hit or miss method, basing the order of choices solely on the comparative rotundity of females. We introduce the fattest female that has shed most recently into a male's cage to gauge his reaction. If she's ready to be bred, she'll be emitting a powerful pheromone – kind of a chemical perfume - that excites males into a vigorous urge to copulate. We feel that it's the male's job to notice this and initiate the action, so we don't want to move him out of the familiar surroundings of his cage as a possible distraction. Other successful breeders use the opposite approach based on the reckoning that it's the males that are less distracted by foreign territory because they do the most wandering in search of mates. The reality is that it probably doesn't make much difference either way - when they're ready to mate, not much will deter them from their goal.

Misting the enclosure and its occupants with an atomizer bottle of room temperature water instantly raises the humidity, which enhances the spread and recognition of the female's chemical love potion. We also, whenever convenient, arrange to introduce snakes on warm, humid evenings when they would naturally be indulging in such activities in the wild. Approaching storm fronts that lower the barometric pressure seem to stimulate increased breeding excitement in corns.

At this point, all that's necessary is to stand back and observe. The male will usually take an immediate interest in any new snake in his territory. His first task is to determine its sex, usually by crawling forward and examining it with his tongue. He'll often move in a series of spasmodic, jerking pulses. He takes particular interest in the cloacal region where the sex organs presumably are most detectable by scent or pheromones. The reaction to another male is swift, consisting of violent pushing and bumping and sometimes biting him along the body. This is not to be confused with the love bites of male-female courtship described below. Two male snakes may thrash about the enclosure in a contest of strength, or one will try to escape frantically. While this may be good exercise, we recommend separating the introduced male and admitting that someone made a mistake sexing it. Try another prospective mate right away while your main male is primed for action.

Upon checking out the introduced snake and discovering that it's really a female, if the time is right, the male will rub his chin along her length, often accompanying this with an undulating wave motion of his body while lining himself up parallel to her. He'll attempt to line up their tails, sliding his under hers to lift it for easier access to her cloacal opening. Depending on her degree of cooperation, she may lift her tail and gape her cloaca open in a display we call 'flagging' – certainly an obvious invitation to mate when she's at her height of readiness. Males also occasionally gently bite the heads or necks of females during courtship, but they never bite with a violent chewing motion as when attacking a rival male.

Males have a pair of sex organs, each of which is called a hemipenis (the plural is *hemipenes*). They normally lie inverted inside the base of the tail just posterior to the vent. When the cloacal openings are lined up facing one another, a sudden pulse pushes one hemipenis into the female. It only takes a split second and may easily be missed until you've seen it happen a few times. Upon careful inspection, a small area of the hemipenis may be visible where the cloacas are joined. The tails typically rise upward, partly intertwined and almost side by side after a moment. The pair stays locked in this position, almost motionless except for an occasional spasmodic twitch, for about ten to 20 minutes on average. They then quietly disengage and go their separate ways. This is sometimes initiated by one starting to leave the scene by dragging its still-connected mate for a short distance.

It's important for us to know exactly when, or if, each of our females is bred because we conduct numerous breedings designed to cross specific traits. Due to the speed of the whole mating affair, and the fact that we're often working on dozens of pairs simultaneously, it's sometimes difficult to monitor the progress in every cage. The simple matter of using plain paper or newsprint as a temporary cage substrate has two related advantages. It can be inspected for semen after the mating attempt since a small, yellowish viscous spillage nearly always follows a successful breeding episode. This sperm spill is more noticeable on paper than mulch, and a non-polluted sample can be obtained for microscopic sperm viability analysis if desired.

We've found that allowing males a minimal three-day rest period before being called for stud service again seems adequate to give them time to build up enough sperm for further fertile breedings. Larger, older males seem to recover and are ready to breed again sooner than younger, less-seasoned ones. Fully mature males may also be capable of more fertile breedings per season. Small first-timer males often seem to deplete their sperm after their first one or two matings, and continued copulations result in a rapidly declining fertility rate in the females they breed.

One mating is all that's usually necessary to achieve successful fertilization, but there's no harm in letting a female mate as many times as she wants if you have enough males to spare. Short-term sperm storage is a documented phenomenon in many snake species that allows females to hold viable sperm for weeks or months until they're ready to ovulate. Only at that (often later) time does actual fertilization occur. This is important to note since it alters the expected gestation period, making the egg deposition date harder to predict. We maintain a ratio of approximately one male for every four to six females, estimating that this is a reasonable number which a healthy, large male *guttata* can service comfortably per season. You may certainly exceed this ratio in a pinch, or you may mate a female with many different males if knowing the genetic heritage of the offspring is unimportant to you.

GESTATION AND EGG-LAYING

Gravid females usually continue to feed ravenously for an additional three to five weeks after mating before the enlarging eggs in the oviducts make passing food or fecal matter uncomfortable. Appetites will slacken or quit completely as the females approach their pre-natal shed, which is a clue that egg-laying will occur in about 10 to 14 days. You may still offer food, noting that much smaller than usual items are more readily accepted and are less stressful to digest at this point. Females are literally bulging by then, and have a distinctive pudgy feeling to their rear halves.

Just before the prenatal shed is the time to prepare a nesting container for the female. Gravid corns seek out a secret, sheltered place with high humidity to deposit a clutch of eggs. If they can't find a suitable spot, they'll drop the eggs in the closest thing available – in a dry hide-box or in the water bowl, both of which may spell death for the eggs. Translucent plastic food storage tubs with snap-on lids have proven to be ideally suited for our nest box needs. Not only are they moisture-proof; they also allow easy visual checking without removing the snake if she's coiled inside. A single round entrance hole about twice the female's widest diameter is cut in the top of a box that has the capacity to hold at least two snakes the size of your female. Use a box with plenty of floor area rather than one that's mostly vertical space.

Some kind of moistened material should fill one-half to two-thirds of the box to help create an inviting lair. Female corns like to burrow into the substrate and shove it aside to form a nesting cavity, as opposed to laying eggs in a large open space that they may perceive has room for a predator to enter. We've had long-term success using dampened sphagnum moss, although moist vermiculite or crumpled paper towels are fine too. As long as whatever you use lacks a strong odor and holds moisture, it should work fine. Place it in the cage when you first notice the female's eyes clouding because she may find it convenient for loosening her skin preparatory to the pre-natal shed. It will also be a familiar retreat later when she would have to otherwise search for a good place to lay her eggs.

Our corns have generally laid their eggs from 31 to 45 days after mating, averaging about 39 days. This is one to two weeks after their pre-natal shed (the one just prior to laying eggs). Many keepers use that shed as their cue to place a nest box in the cage, although we have had one bloodline that includes females that routinely lay *during* the height of their blue-eyed stage prior to shedding. They may be quite active the few days prior to deposition if they haven't yet chosen the nesting site. Once they've picked it though, they seem content to relax and wait, usually inside the container and as out of sight as possible. They may lay the clutch any time of night or day, and the process may span from an hour or two to a couple days in abnormal cases (see egg-binding in PROBLEMS). The eggs are soft and wet at deposition, with the shells drying and adhering to those beside them over the next several hours.

The mother often remains in the box with the egg mass in a semi-lethargic state. We disturb her as little as possible when we take the mass away, although we know that females show little resistance to this act aside from some minor shoving with their coils. If she's extremely thin, the female is offered one or two fuzzy mice, smaller than

The eggs on the left side healthy fertile eggs, fully filled out and dry-shelled. The smaller ones on the right are infertile judging by their smaller relative size and wet appearance.

her own diameter, right away for a snack as a tiny boost before her eyes go opaque again. Most females have a post-laying shed in about ten days and resume feeding normally almost immediately afterward. Occasionally the strain of carrying eggs wears down a female so much that she has difficulty recovering weight or even holding down meals she normally could handle with ease. We isolate and nurse such specimens with a series of smaller food items, especially thawed fuzzy mice, for ease of digestion until they recover.

We've had clutches with as few as four or five eggs from very small first-time female corns. There was a case in June 1999, as this book was in preparation, documented with photos by Karen and Joe Street, of a five-year-old amelanistic corn they had raised laying 53 eggs in one clutch. The snake is husky but only about 4 ½ feet (137 cm) in length. Her eggs were slightly smaller than usual, and all but one or two appeared to be fertile. She has a track record of losing little weight and recovering quickly to double clutch, and was expected to do so again. This same female, in the 1997 breeding season, first laid 40 eggs and later laid a second clutch of 35 eggs. All 75 eggs hatched and thrived. The largest clutch produced from a wild-collected specimen of which we are aware came from Lee County,

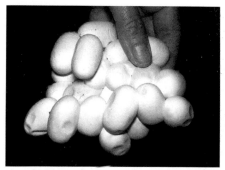

A clump of normal corn snake eggs typically adheres firmly together in a mass within a couple hours of being laid.

Florida and was acquired gravid by Mark Pellicer. It laid 45 eggs in one clutch on May 23, 1984, and all 45 eggs hatched out as healthy neonates.

Young or undersized specimens of many colubrid species tend to lay low numbers of physically large eggs. After their second or third year of production, they settle into the routine of laying clutches based more on their individual genetics, with a tendency for the number of eggs in clutches to slowly but steadily accrue with females' increasing age. The quality and quantity of their diet for the months preceding breeding may also affect the number of eggs and/or the size of each egg.

Healthy (fertile) eggs are an opaque white or slightly yellowish-white, oblong to nearly round, and from ¾ to 1 ½ inches (1.9–3.8 cm) in length. Infertile or otherwise compromised eggs are usually smaller, yellower, and often retain a wet appearance by their failure to absorb moisture normally. They often don't stick to the others, instead tending to roll away and sit alone. Good eggs are generally smooth and absorb moisture on their shells. They frequently have, or end up with, numerous irregularities such as rough starburst-like patches, clearish "windows," stains, discolorations, and oddly rounded shapes on their ends. Most of these are inconsequential and may reflect some imbalance in vitamin/ mineral ratios in the mothers' diets. If eggs with such defects otherwise seem healthy, there's no reason to try to separate them right away; leaving them in the clump is fine.

Corn eggs can be candled in much the same way that is used for birds' eggs. The simple technique involves focusing a beam of bright, cool light against the shell. Special devices are sold for this purpose, but the same advantageous effect they offer can be easily duplicated by rolling a dark piece of paper around a flashlight and projecting it while the egg is held at the end of the tube. View the egg from the side opposite the light beam, or from a 90° angle depending upon the intensity of your light source. Look for evidence of blood vessels inside as it glows, which are a sure sign of fertile development proceeding.

This snow corn has just laid a modest-sized clutch of eggs that have spread out in the oversized nest box using vermiculite as the moist substrate medium. Note the tiny, yellow, obviously infertile eggs off to the side.

INCUBATION OF EGGS

Corns in the wild deposit their eggs out of sight in holes in the ground, in piles of leaves, or in the wood mulch within dead trees. We try to mimic that arrangement by burying the eggs in an incubation medium in a shoebox or other moisture-retentive container that has at least enough depth to accommodate the clutch, with an additional inch or more to spare on all sides. A container that closes completely, like a plastic shoebox, works well to reduce the drying effect of breezes. Only a few scattered pinholes in its walls and lid are needed to let enough oxygen in so that the eggs can breathe. The main goal is maintaining a high ambient humidity close to, but not quite at, 100% since eggs are mostly water themselves. Their semi-porous leathery shells gain or lose moisture as needed, so keeping their surroundings humid allows them to maintain their relative equilibrium easily.

Many materials work adequately as incubation media. Our two personal favorites are sphagnum moss and coarse vermiculite, both obtainable wherever plant nursery supplies are sold. Both media allow oxygen to circulate next to the shells while also keeping them moist as water diffuses through them. We have a slight preference for sphagnum moss since its fluffy composition better accommodates the vertical clumps of eggs that corn snakes usually deposit. We soak it thoroughly, and then wring it out as completely as possible by hand to start with about the correct level of dampness. The eggs are completely buried in it so none are visible without lifting up a one to two inch thick "pad" of moss to expose them underneath. This envelops the entire clutch in a moist yet airy medium so some portions of the shells don't dry and harden, which can make hatching difficult later. Sphagnum

A 'Bloodred' is about to pass her last egg of the clutch, which can be seen as the bulge near her cloaca. Except for snapping this photo, we would normally never disturb a female during this sensitive time.

contains tannic acid that leaves harmless brown stains on the shells, but its acidic pH is beneficial because it retards bacterial growth.

Combining vermiculite with an equal weight of water will achieve a similarly appropriate mixture. The large-granule kind with particles approximately 1/8 inch (3-4 mm) in width is best to allow air-flow through it. Its sterile, non-organic make-up also discourages fungi and bacteria unless deteriorating eggs themselves invite attack. Vermiculite works particularly well when the clump of eggs is relatively flat and spread out horizontally, or if many are separated and can be buried individually so that only 10% of the shell is visible. This keeps the threat of desiccation low, yet also leaves a tiny patch in view to periodically monitor for any which might go bad. Rob MacInnes taught me a simple trick that works particularly nicely with vermiculite: lay a single sheet of newspaper or paper towel, cut to cover the surface area of the egg container, loosely on top of the contents. Check the eggs every four to seven days by lifting the paper out to peek at the eggs' condition, at the same time assessing the paper's degree of moistness with your bare fingers. If it's hard and crinkly, or the eggs have sunken indentations, add water to the vermiculite around the outer edges of the container away from the eggs. If the paper is wet or slimy and/or the eggs seem swollen to bursting and feel unusually turgid, it's time to reduce the humidity. Leave the container lid off for a few hours to let evaporation dry it out a little, and replace some of the wet medium with fresh dry vermiculite.

Most people use incubators to assure relatively even temperature gradients and protect eggs against nighttime lows. The complexities of incubators run the gamut from homemade designs using old aquariums and heating pads (*not* advised!) to technological marvels designed for laboratories or adapted from medical incubators which cost thousands of dollars. Our experience with a simple 18 inch (46 cm) square by 8 inch (20 cm) high model made of styrofoam, called the Hova-Bator™ and made for poultry eggs, has been excellent. Most agricultural feed and supply stores sell them for about $50, as do many mail-order herp dealers. Smaller individual egg containers, such as margarine or deli meal tubs or trays, as opposed to shoeboxes, fit better within such units and keep clutches separate. Alternately, the entire floor of the incubator can be covered in sphagnum or vermiculite and the eggs put directly into it without additional holding containers.

With so many other variables between models, our only piece of broadly applicable (and hard-earned) advice is to spend a couple days setting the unit, with a quantity of moist incubation medium in place to hold heat, *days before* any eggs are trusted to it. The styrofoam models described above do *not* have a simple calibrated adjustment knob, so repeated trial and error micro-adjustments are necessary at first, only a 1 or 2% turn of the angled metal knob each time. Once set, be careful to never bump the knob. On any type of incubator, use a good mercury thermometer (the Hova-Bator comes with a hard-to-read but accurate small one) to check temps, with the ball end buried an inch into the medium which the eggs will soon occupy. That way it's not subject to radical changes when the unit is opened during inspections, letting a puff of cooler air rush in that would otherwise give you a false reading.

Mold and mildew occasionally develop on the shells of eggs. White, fuzzy kinds may be an indication of too much humidity and/or lack of fresh air circulation. It's easily remedied by opening the container and allowing it to dry out somewhat, and by also adding more ventilation holes to the incubation container. You should fluff the incubation medium to let some air get into it, and loosen the eggs themselves if they're 'stuck' in damp pockets within the material. At that point, it won't hurt to also manually rinse the eggs under room temperature water and pat them dry with paper towels.

When green or blue molds appear on eggs within the first two weeks after deposition, it has been, in our experience, a herald of dying eggs. Application of anti-fungal powders, such as clotrimazole (Lotrimin®) for athlete's foot, has been used successfully to salvage eggs under attack. Swabbing the bad areas with a Listerine™-moistened Q-tip also works. This is especially useful when eggs reach maximum swelling just prior to hatching and develop problems at poorly calcified areas that rupture prematurely. Be careful not to turn the eggs from their original upright positions as they're treated or cleaned. If the colors return quickly, you're free to try whatever you think may work because those eggs are almost certainly lost. Sniffing them for a rotten smell will usually confirm it. It's best to separate these bad eggs from any good ones to avoid possible contamination, if you don't risk breaking good eggs by doing so. If you do deem separation necessary, carefully cut the infected one(s) away with blunt-nosed bandage scissors, and sop up any residual fluids from the part remaining adhered to the good eggs.

Cutting away bad eggs is not always necessary. Water sprayed at the junction points will help loosen eggs from the main mass as the offending egg is slowly flexed loose with your fingers, especially in recently laid clutches. Do not use any chemical disinfectants or other potentially noxious fluids that may be absorbed by the good eggs. If any eggs must be moved from their original resting places, we suggest marking the uppermost surfaces lightly with a pencil (*not* a marker with wet ink) so they can be replaced with the same side facing up. This precaution is to avoid "drowning" a developing baby by rotating its head into a lower position within the embryonic fluid. Eggs never have to contend with rotation during normal incubation in the wild.

Healthy eggs have fully filled-out shells for the majority of their development, only losing their turgidity and collapsing slightly in the last few days before hatching. They actually grow, gaining nearly half again their original diameter at laying over the next two months. Bigger, heavier babies hatch from eggs kept fully hydrated. If they appear to dent inward or shrink at any time before the eighth week has passed, the eggs are dehydrating and need to absorb water. The situation is remedied (if the eggs have not sunken in by more than about 40%) by

Two ways of setting up eggs is demonstrated: The clumped eggs on the left are surrounded by a mound of damp sphagnum moss to better cover the adherent vertical pile. On the right, eggs that are not stuck to each other are mostly buried in moist, large-grained vermiculite and covered with a sheet of paper to hold in and gauge humidity levels.

wetting the medium adjoining the eggs for quick diffusion into them and to boost the general humidity of the box. For a faster fix of severe problems, mist the eggs directly, using water the same temperature as the incubator to avoid temperature shock. Cover the eggs immediately afterward to avoid cooling from evaporation. These salvage tactics should be tried on all dehydrated eggs, no matter how bad they look, in case they can be saved despite a hopelessly shriveled appearance.

It's not uncommon for a small percentage of eggs to spoil during incubation, often for no apparent reason. Don't despair – that's why corn snakes lay lots of them! A final hatch rate of 85-95% is quite good overall in a large collection, although the usual situation in our collection is for *most* clutches to hatch nearly 100% and for a few entire clutches to die and be lost completely. A bad egg virtually never affects the healthy ones attached to it, even if it turns into a kaleidoscope of colored molds or becomes covered in bugs or maggots. We agree with the old assertion that "good eggs don't go bad" and thus aren't really prone to attack by something that was only taking advantage of eggs dying anyway.

Elaphe guttata eggs hatch in approximately nine weeks at their optimal hatching temperature of 85°F (29.5°C), but there's a lot of leeway in this very <u>un</u>critical figure. One record was sent to us of a clutch of 17 eggs that resulted in only one live baby hatching 120 days after laying, which

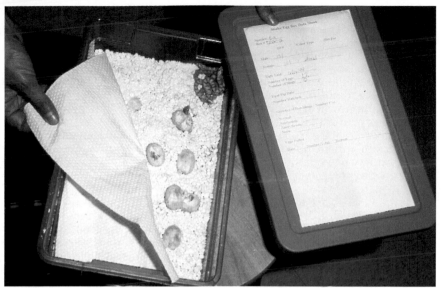

Amelanistic corns are hatching from eggs incubated in perlite, a soil lightening granulated additive that some breeders prefer. The lowest half-inch of this material may have standing water that evaporates up through it to maintain a high ambient humidity without the actual surface of the eggs coming in contact with wet pieces of the medium.

Normal (left) and anerythristic (right) hatchlings emerging from a clutch of eggs. Note the many slits in the shells made by their egg teeth as they worked to slice suitable exit openings.

is abnormally long. A range of incubation temperatures, from 70°F (21°C) to 90°F (32°C), is well tolerated, especially if those extremes only represent fluctuations over the course of the day and not the average for most of it. Hundreds of clutches of corn eggs have hatched for us over the past few years after an average of 73 days of incubation time (the actual range was between 69 and 80 days) using only the "room temperature method." Hazardous temperatures lurk closer to the high end than the low, with exposure to over 92°F (33.3°C) for even an hour sometimes proving fatal to eggs. Within the safe zone, we'd narrow the range down to 82-88°F (28-31°C) for best results. This range will hatch corn eggs in approximately 52-59 days depending upon how accurately it stays at any given point on that scale. Cooler or slightly warmer averages can slow or speed up the time by a week or more.

We actually feel that moderate temperature fluctuations may be beneficial, in a not yet fully comprehended way. Certain functions of embryonic development may progress most properly in the mildly varying temperatures that eggs experience under unstable natural conditions. In southern Florida, we achieve a safe range by merely letting eggs sit at room temperatures (70°-90°F) for our latitude from May through September. Most people though will opt to use an incubator set to maintain an exact reading that doesn't deviate by more than a couple degrees.

Eggs often develop longitudinal "hairline cracks" or "stretch marks," and virtually always dimple inward during the three to six days prior to hatching. This is normal as yolk is being absorbed into the snakelings' bodies, so don't try to inflate them with a spraying from the mist bottle at this time. Soon, tiny slits start appearing, mostly in the upward-facing portions of the shells. They're formed by tiny egg-puncturing "teeth" that temporarily grace hatchlings' snouts for that purpose. Heads then protrude (this stage is called 'pipping') and often pause for minutes or hours as this resting period prepares babies for their final thrust into a new, uncertain world. Some breeders routinely make a starter incision in the shells of any eggs that haven't pipped within 24–48 hours of the first one, to help weak babies escape from particularly tough or thick-shelled eggs. When they finally emerge completely, they're glossy wet and about 10-12 inches (25–33 cm) long on average. We've heard of hatchlings as small as eight inches (20 cm).

Neonates even smaller than eight inches have emerged from single eggs as twins. Two sets of twins, one of them involving a normal and an anerythristic baby from a single egg (obviously fraternal twins in this case) were hatched in 1998 by Adrian Hemens. The parental stock that produced them shared a recent common ancestor, a hint that the tendency for twinning may be heritable. All four neonates fed voluntarily and thrived. Bicephalism (having two heads) is believed to be an incomplete effort at twinning and has also occurred in corns. Few have survived more than a few months, the exception being a female hatched in 1981 and raised by Craig Trumbower to adulthood. This hardy specimen accepted food readily from both heads equally, finally attaining a length of nearly five feet. She was never involved in successful reproductive efforts.

HOUSING NEONATES

Neonates typically explore their surroundings for several minutes after leaving their shells before seeking cover under anything in the container. When we check for hatchlings in clear shoeboxes, we often first lift the box and look up at the bottom from below. If some or all of the eggs have hatched, the neonates are usually jumbled together on the bottom in one corner and are easily spotted. Normally an entire clutch will hatch within about 36 hours of one another. Unequal heat distribution during incubation may cause a greater range of time, the warmer eggs being the first to pip.

Plastic shoeboxes make ideal starter cages for baby corns. They're cheap, readily available, and the lids either snap down securely or can be held tight with a weight placed upon them. The most common shoeboxes are about 6 ½ x 12 x 3 ¾ inches high (16 x 30 x 9.5 cm high) and can house a corn comfortably for a half year or longer, depending on growth rate, until it attains a length of 18-20 inches (48-51 cm). Substrates can range from a single layer of paper towel or newspaper to shredded aspen. We recommend avoiding aspen for a month or two until the snakes are feeding easily. Sometimes babies have to struggle while learning to subdue their first meals, and they may accidentally ingest pieces of particulate substrate in the process. One-piece substrates eliminate this hazard and are also easy to check for other signs of trouble, such as abnormal feces, regurgitated food, or uneaten pinkies, during the early stages of acclimation.

For the first few months after hatching, some large-scale breeders have housed their baby corns directly in 4 inch (10 cm) diameter deli cups. This has the advantage over shoeboxes of saving storage space, and the same cup can later be used for shipping the specimen it formerly housed. The baby mice offered as food are also found readily by the snakes in such close quarters, resulting in a higher percentage starting to feed voluntarily this way. On the down side, the deli cup necessitates finding small enough containers to serve as water bowls. PVC plastic pipe caps are most often used, but with no room for a hiding place too, the snakes frequently coil in the water, spilling it. Excess moisture build-up can quickly lead to fungus infections in hot, humid climates, particularly when a snake is confined virtually on top of its own feces. Cleaning must be a bi-weekly chore minimally for specimens held this way temporarily.

BREEDING CHARTS

The following reproductive data were tabulated for a large colony of corn snakes, managed intensively for maximum offspring over the three-year period spanning 1997-1999. The information clearly illustrates the potential productivity of *Elaphe guttata* on the level of a mass farming operation.

1997 BREEDING SEASON RESULTS

TOTAL 1st clutches produced from 250 female corns judged as breedable-sized adults: 232
Percentage of females laying 1st clutches: . . . . .93.0 %
TOTAL 1st clutch eggs ("good" + slugs): 3866
Total # of eggs looking "good" at laying time: 3205
Percentage of "good" eggs at laying time: . . . . .82.9 %
1st clutch – average # of all eggs per clutch: 16.7
1st clutch – average # of "good" eggs per clutch, judged at the time of laying : 13.8
1st clutch – average # of eggs actually hatching successfully per clutch: 12.8

TOTAL 2nd clutches produced: 211
Percentage of females laying 2nd clutches: . . . . 84.4 %
TOTAL 2nd clutch eggs ("good" + slugs): 2545
Total # of eggs looking "good" at laying time: 1652
Percentage of "good" eggs at laying time: . . . . 64.9 %
2nd clutch – average # of all eggs per clutch: 12.0
2nd clutch – average # of "good" eggs per clutch, judged at the time of laying : 7.8
2nd clutch – average # of eggs actually hatching successfully per clutch: 6.6

(3 females laid 3rd clutches with an average of
only 2 viable eggs per clutch from nearly 14 each.)

Per female annual production.
Average # of total eggs per female for all 1997: 25.8
Average # of "good" eggs per female for 1997: 19.5
Average # of clutches per female for 1997: 1.78

In 1997, 250 females within the colony were deemed safely breedable by size, based on weight alone when each one was 7 ounces (200 grams) or more. In 1998 and 1999, the minimum breeding weight per female was raised to 8.5 ounces (240 grams), with allowances made for certain husky but slightly smaller individuals, based on personal inspection. Many females were well above minimal size during all seasons' trials, of course. It should also be noted that this commercial enterprise was striving for quantities of hatchlings, so females were heavily fed and bred again after their first clutches were laid to produce the high percentages of second clutches noted.

1998 BREEDING SEASON RESULTS

TOTAL 1st clutches produced from 262 female corns judged as breedable-sized adults: . 260
Percentage of females laying 1st clutches: . . . . 99.2 %
TOTAL 1st clutch eggs ("good" + slugs): 5056
Total # of eggs looking "good" at laying time: 4460
Percentage of "good" eggs at laying time: . . . . 88.2 %
1st clutch – average # of all eggs per clutch: 19.5
1st clutch – average # of "good" eggs per clutch, judged at the time of laying : 17.2
1st clutch – average # of eggs actually hatching successfully per clutch: 17.0

TOTAL 2nd clutches produced: 207
Percentage of females laying 2nd clutches: . . . . 79.0 %
TOTAL 2nd clutch eggs ("good" + slugs): 2447
Total # of eggs looking "good" at laying time: 1041
Percentage of "good" eggs at laying time: . . . . 42.5 %

2nd clutch – average # of all eggs per clutch: 11.8
2nd clutch – average # of "good" eggs per clutch, judged at the time of laying : 5.0
2nd clutch – average # of eggs actually hatching successfully per clutch: 4.0

(No 3rd clutches were produced in the 1998 season.)

Per female annual production
Average # of total eggs per female for all 1998: 28.6
Average # of "good" eggs per female for 1998: 21.0
Average # of clutches per female for 1998: 1.78

These data clearly demonstrate that corns are quite capable of double clutching. However, both the numbers of good eggs and the percentages of eggs that appear fertile at deposition drop with the second effort in a single season. The two consecutive years' figures also indicate that not using barely minimum-sized females is a wise breeding strategy. Many of the females involved in this study had been in the colony double clutching for two to three years prior to 1997. Virtually all of them recovered their weight and continued to grow in size, leading to the belief that this level of production is quite sustainable over many years. The large-scale figures for this statistically significant information is presented courtesy of Bill Brant and Joe Hiduke of *The Gourmet Rodent*, Archer, Florida.

1999 BREEDING SEASON RESULTS

TOTAL 1st clutches produced from 504 female corns judged as breedable-sized adults: 489
Percentage of females laying 1st clutches: . . . . 97.0 %
TOTAL 1st clutch eggs ("good" + slugs): 8563
Total # of eggs looking "good" at laying time: 7683
Percentage of "good" eggs at laying time: . . . . 89.7 %
1st clutch – average # of all eggs per clutch: 17.5
1st clutch – average # of "good" eggs per clutch, judged at the time of laying : 15.7
1st clutch – average # of eggs actually hatching successfully per clutch: 13.3

TOTAL 2nd clutches produced: 408
Percentage of females laying 2nd clutches: . . . . 81.0 %
TOTAL 2nd clutch eggs ("good" + slugs): 4850
Total # of eggs looking "good" at laying time: 3130
Percentage of "good" eggs at laying time: . . . . 64.5 %
2nd clutch – average # of all eggs per clutch: 11.9
2nd clutch – average # of "good" eggs perclutch, judged at the time of laying : 7.7
2nd clutch – average # of eggs actually hatching successfully per clutch: 6.6

(No 3rd clutches were produced in the 1999 season.)

Per female annual production
Average # of total eggs per female for all 1999: . . 26.6
Average # of "good" eggs per female for 1999: . . 21.4
Average # of clutches per female for 1999: 1.81

These data clearly demonstrate that corns are quite capable of producing multiple fertile clutches of eggs per year. However, both the percentages of eggs that appear fertile at deposition time, and those that hatch, usually drop with the second effort in a single occasion. Intense sustained reproduction like this requires heavy feeding and superb care to maintain the health of females and allow them to build up weight to breed again the following year.

The colony's diminished success percentages, despite overall increased numbers in 1999, is attributed to the near doubling of the number of females in the colony with the addition of a large number of 1-year-old females breeding for the first time at minimal adult size. Also of significance was the fact that the majority of the new females were *not* selected for their prolific heritage as had been policy in the past, but rather to introduce a variety of new colors and patterns. The large-scale figures for this statistically significant information are presented courtesy of Bill Brant and Joe Hiduke of *The Gourmet Rodent*, Archer, Florida.

These data clearly demonstrate that corns are quite capable of double clutching. However, both the numbers of good eggs and the percentages of eggs that appear fertile at deposition drop with the second effort in a single season. The three consecutive years' figures also indicate that not using barely minimum-sized females is a wise breeding strategy. Many of the females involved in this study had been in the colony double clutching for two to three years prior to 1997. Virtually all of them recovered their weight and continued to grow in size, leading to the belief that this level of production is quite sustainable over many years. The large-scale figures for this statistically significant information is presented courtesy of Bill Brant and Joe Hiduke of The Gourmet Rodent, Archer, Florida.

Occasionally snakes that appear to be swollen and obviously gravid never lay eggs, either eating the clutch or reabsorbing them. The latter is probably the correct, but confusing reality. Snakes can absorb unfertilized ova back into their bodies, but not fertile developing eggs. The problem in such a case is likely to be the male's - he may have physically copulated with the female, but did not actually impregnate her with viable sperm. If she ovulated later, *after* mating, which is common in captivity, the bulging of her belly from ovulation might have occurred about the time you expected her to start looking gravid. This has fooled many keepers into thinking a clutch of eggs is imminent, only to be disappointed as the weeks pass and the female slowly regains her normal appearance. But if the eggs were never in fact fertilized at all, they would just be reabsorbed into her body with no trace left behind. We've never heard of proof of corns swallowing their own eggs and doubt the plausibility of that explanation in most instances of reabsorption.

LUNAR versus REPRODUCTIVE CYCLES

Breeding cycles which are synchronized with lunar (moon) cycles are well-documented occurrences in lower lifeforms. It's unreasonable to assume that lunar cycles don't also have an effect upon corn snakes, and seasoned breeders swear that in fact the cycles do, though the opinions are based mostly on gut instincts. We graphed data from our written records for all female corns breeding during the 1997 and 1998 seasons, looking for correlations of reproduction with specific phases of the moon. The breeding dates were biased since *we* are the ones who chose them, although those decisions were based on females' relative states of readiness to breed in our estimation. Even considering that bias, we saw a tendency for egg-laying dates to cluster around the full moons that occurred between late May and early June of those years. Hatching dates showed much more sprawl over time, and thus less correlation with lunar cycles. These data are very preliminary, and are presented just to stimulate thought.

PART III DISEASES and DISORDERS

Besides the problems discussed earlier under shedding and breeding, corns are subject to the same array of disorders that can affect many kinds of snakes. In their defense, we must emphasize that *Elaphe guttata* is among the hardiest of all snakes kept as pets today. Captive-raised specimens especially have a rather low probability of suffering from any of these maladies. We've chosen to discuss them in descending order of likelihood (except for the final one) based on our years of dealing with tens of thousands of individuals. This section is more like a "First Aid" course on this topic - **we urge you to seek the aid of a qualified veterinarian for serious problems that do not respond to the basic treatments we've outlined.** The veterinary reference books listed in back are also excellent and very current in their more in-depth discussions of these subjects.

EXTERNAL PARASITES

Mites
Mites are pinhead-size (1 mm) arachnids, most often noticed bulging like tiny balloons from the skin of your snakes. They also appear as tiny black or red 'beads' crawling around over snakes' bodies. Mites feed upon blood, which they extract by their sucking mouth parts while imbedded between scales. Red mites infest wild snakes mostly and have never plagued captive collections after being initially removed. The black ones, the common snake mite *Ophionyssus natricis*, are slightly larger and evolved to parasitize herps as adults. These mites multiply rapidly and can cause lethargy, dehydration, or anemia in their victims when present in large numbers. Their travels throughout a collection can also make them important vectors of disease.

If unsure of a mite infestation, first check the water bowl for dead ones that fall in and drown. Their bodies look like grains of coarse pepper on the bottom of the bowl. Another simple test is to let the snake in question crawl through your snuggly clenched fist so that it rubs its entire length against your fingers. This will almost surely dislodge some mites onto your skin, where they're easily seen as they move about. Also look for them around snakes' eyes, in the mental (chin) groove, and between all the large head scales. Snake mites don't bite people, so they're not a personal concern to handlers. Do the examination over a sink so your hands, fingernails, etc. can be washed on the spot, and the snake rinsed off to start the removal process immediately if necessary. Severe infestations of black snake mites may actually give the snake itself a peppered appearance or a "salted" one if the whitish feces have accumulated in sufficient quantities.

Mites are easy to kill on any particular snake, but more difficult to eradicate from a collection or room. Regardless of the extermination methods used on the snake, resign yourself to soaking all cages and cage furniture, dipping them in a strong (10% or greater) liquid chlorine and water solution for at least ten minutes. If all particulate matter is brushed out first, this should let the bleach reach all parts of the cage and kill all eggs and hidden mites. An old method of treatment is to place the snake in a plastic shoe box (small snakes) or sweater box half filled with water. The lid should be perforated to allow for air flow and weighted down or taped shut. This will drown most mites. Monitor snakes during this process and remove them after an hour. A few drops of liquid soap added to the soaking water reduces the water tension, which cuts down on air pockets under and around snakes' scales and drowns mites more quickly. The only drawback is that some will migrate up to the head and survive. These can be manually removed under a rushing spigot, or by gentle rubbing with a damp cloth. A dab of petroleum jelly over a snake's eye will suffocate mites buried around the ocular scale.

An ivermectin spray consisting of 5-10 mg of liquid ivermectin to a quart or liter of water can be applied directly to snakes and their cages (minus the water bowl) to destroy mites. It's best to repeat the spraying weekly for several weeks to get all stragglers. We have used a "shake and bake" method in which a snake is dusted inside a bag of dry 5% or 10% Sevin® dust. This product is sold in botanical nurseries to control plant pests, but it's *not* officially sanctioned for use in snakes. In our experience, Sevin® dust appears to be harmless to snakes if not ingested or left clogging their mouths, nostrils, or vent. We wash specimens off thoroughly after the treatment, and then we take the additional precautionary step of scattering some Sevin dust on the shelves and floor to prevent odd mites from migrating around the area.

Airborne insecticides such as "pest strips" with Vapona™ (2,2-dichlorovinyl dimethyl phosphate) kill mites without the mess, but are tricky to gauge for the dosage delivered or received. They can be especially dangerous when used to treat juvenile snakes which have a lower threshold of tolerance to this toxin than adults. In early trials, we inadvertently overdosed baby corns by leaving them exposed to a 1 by 3 inch piece of pest strip for only one hour in a shoebox with only a couple ventilation holes. The snakes suffered neurological damage that caused them to permanently lose the ability to crawl normally. They also went into a "stargazing" behavior in which they bend their heads backward as if dizzy or disoriented and a couple died within one day. We urge caution when using pest strips with juvenile corn snakes.

For a cage 12 x 30 x 12 inches high (30 x 76 x 30 cm high), we now put a piece measuring 1 x 2 inches (2.5 x 5 cm), cut from a fresh yellow strip, on top of the cage lid or against a wall vent. Remove the water bowl so there's no chance of any of the impregnated chemical in the strip dissolving out of the air into the water. Lay a piece of newspaper *loosely* over the main cage vents or screen lid, making sure that some air is still getting by. The idea is to slow air exchange by cutting breezes but not to seal the cage off completely. Leave it like this, checking for signs of mites still alive after 24 hours. If any are found, repeat the procedure, possibly increasing the "dosage" by using a second piece of pest strip, and/or blocking air exchange somewhat more completely. Save the pieces of strips in a tightly sealed jar. Mites can hatch, grow to adulthood, and reproduce within two weeks at 86°F (30°C). Repeating the procedure weekly for at least several weeks after the last sign of mites, specifically to kill any residual mite eggs in the cage that hatch later, is necessary to work toward permanently eliminating the problem. We've found that strips that have a greenish tinge, either when first unsealed or later, do not work effectively.

Caution: Treating snakes that are "in shed" is not recommended. There may be a greater risk for pesticide absorption as well as unnecessary damage to the skin when handling. Also, do not combine multiple chemical treatments at the same time.

Ticks

Ticks are usually brown to grey, and from 1/16 to 3/16 inch (2-6 mm) in length when they first appear attached by their mouths to an area between or partially under snakes' scales. They stay in place and slowly expand as they suck blood, occasionally reaching ½ inch (12 mm) or more in diameter when fully engorged. They're mostly a concern on wild-caught snakes and aren't predisposed to making an ongoing nuisance of themselves in captivity. When outbreaks occur on a caged snake, they can usually be attributed to the sudden growth of a group of tiny immature ticks that went undetected earlier on a recently collected specimen. The same methods that rid snakes of mites will kill ticks too, although they often remain embedded in the skin when they die. Simply picking them off with tweezers works well whether they're live or dead. A dab of irritating fluid such as alcohol or ammonia often persuades them to loosen their grip for easier removal. A small gob of Vaseline® over them also works by cutting their oxygen supply and slowly forcing them to release to breathe. Try to get the imbedded mouth parts out too so they are not left in the skin to possibly cause infection.

DIGESTIVE DISORDERS

These encompass an assortment of symptoms including poor appetite, chronic weight loss, wasting away, diarrhea, and stools abnormal in coloration, consistency, or smell. Regurgitation of complete or partially digested food items *may* also be indicative of something more sinister than simple nervousness from lack of a secure hiding place to digest meals or from maintaining animals under too low or high temperatures. Bacterial, protozoan, or viral infections, which require microscopic identification or other diagnostic methods, may require a sample taken from the digestive system of the suspect animal. For proper investigation and identification, growing a culture from the sample in a lab setting may be necessary. Treatments must often be precise in their dosages and timings, and we recommend consulting a qualified reptile veterinarian.
Before assuming the worst, you may want to try the kind and gentle, noninvasive approach of nursing a sick corn back to health. Eliminate as much stress from its life as possible, even if it means not seeing or han-

dling your pet as often as you like. Make sure a temperature gradient exists across the cage that's conducive to proper digestion with a range from 70-88°F (21-31°C). Offer smaller-than-usual and/or previously frozen food items that are easy to break down and absorb by animals below their peaks of vigor. Keep ultra-fresh drinking water available for whenever the debilitated corn wishes to drink.

We've been trying some 'alternative' remedies in recent years. Grapefruit seed extract has been a known suppressor of bacteria in agriculture for a decade and is available for human use at health food stores. A few drops added to the water bowl, after a three-day withholding period to ensure thirst, has yielded encouraging results with young corns prone to regurgitation. Propolis is a proven antimicrobial substance exuded by bees to keep their dark, moist hives free of fungi and germs. It's been used in human medicine for thousands of years by people of other cultures for relief from infections, but it is still largely unfamiliar to many residents of the U.S. We promote continuous experimentation with these "new" medicines to see if they may lead to cures.

INTERNAL PARASITES

Parasites include a wide variety of organisms that cause many of the signs mentioned above. They range from one-celled amoebas and coccidia to tapeworms that can be many times longer than their hosts as they wind through the host's intestine. Protozoa often invade the gut and cling to the walls of the digestive tract where they irritate the lining and lessen the host's ability to absorb nutrients. The larger types of parasites, such as worms and flukes, are mostly a problem of wild-caught specimens that retain parasite loads for long periods after capture. The use of Droncit®, Panacur® or Flagyl® may be warranted. Consult a qualified reptile veterinarian for proper diagnoses and the correct drugs and dosages.

The key to dealing with other gastrointestinal parasites successfully is to first identify the culprit(s). Clues may be found by examining a fecal sample under a microscope to look for the minute organisms, eggs, or even whole worms or pieces of them. Certain larger kinds of parasitic worms like flukes may even be visible clinging inside a snake's mouth as it yawns. Or segments of tapeworms may peek out of the cloaca as the snake defecates. Once an identification is made, a specific vermifuge for that family of parasites probably exists to purge them, even if it is primarily intended for use in large animals of agricultural importance. Some worming medicines can be purchased by anyone at feed/farm supply stores; others will require a prescription by a veterinarian.

To administer vermifuges correctly, the ill snake must be accurately weighed since the amount of cure is often critically linked in a ratio of mgs (milligrams) of medicine per kgs (kilograms) of the patient's body mass. The following drugs and dosages are the most currently recommended by the top vets in the U.S. for the listed parasites. These drug dosages may change as new knowledge accrues, and new drugs will constantly become available, so we cannot over-emphasize the wisdom of consulting an experienced herp veterinarian for professional help in curing snakes with severe cases of these potentially deadly and contagious organisms.

Amoebas and other Protozoans: Metronidazole (Flagyl®) and dimetridazole (Emtryl®) at 50 mg per kg, given orally at two week intervals. It's urgent to clean the snake's cage thoroughly after *every* defecation during the treatment.

Coccidia: Sulphamethazine at 75 mg/kg for the first treatment, then 45 mg/kg over the next five days. (*Cryptosporidium* is a coccidial parasite that's untreatable by present methods.)

Nematodes/Roundworms: Fenbendazole (Panacur®) at 50-100 mg/kg once per week orally for 3-4 weeks duration or Ivermectin at 0.2 mg/kg orally or by injection, repeated in two weeks.

Tapeworms and Flukes: Praziquantel (Droncit®) at 5 mg/kg orally or injected, repeated once after two weeks.

A fecal exam two weeks after the last treatment in any of these cases can be helpful to ensure eradication of these parasites. Many of the dosage regimens used for reptiles are extrapolated from dog and cat research, and are only good estimates.

Today the most dreaded scourge of corn snake collections is the parasite *Cryptosporidium*. It's an invasive protozoan that inhabits the intestinal tract, causing regurgitation and weight loss in infected specimens. A thickening of the stomach, which appears as a midbody swelling in snakes, is a telltale sign in well-advanced stages. Transmission to new hosts is by oral intake of infected liquids, food, or feces. Cryptosporidial disease may kill snakes slowly, in up to two years, thus putting every other animal in a collection at risk of infection. This disease is presently incurable, so specimens harboring it should be completely isolated from all other healthy herps at the very least. Because of *Cryptosporidium*'s extremely infectious nature, experienced collectors recommend destroying infected animals immediately. Veterinarians can perform a screening test involving acid-fast fecal examinations to detect its presence in new specimens before they enter an established herp colony. Several negative fecal results may be necessary to ensure a snake is free of "crypto".

SALMONELLOSIS

Salmonella: Certain strains of this bacteria have been found to be normal gastrointestinal inhabitants in many reptiles and often will not cause disease signs in healthy specimens. However, other pathogenic (illness producing) strains can cause digestive disorders. In captivity, a combination of non-typical or infected foods, the host's inability to self-regulate its environmental conditions such as inadequate temperatures as well as stress, can allow *Salmonella* to build up to excessive levels in the gut. It has long been known to be present in foods for humans, such as raw chicken and eggs, but it can also be transmitted by most other animals.

Signs include bloody diarrhea, weight loss, inactivity and dehydration. Should an animal show signs of disease associated with salmonellosis, then a qualified reptile veterinarian should be consulted for treatment.

Salmonella can be difficult to eradicate in reptiles for several reasons. It is often shed in the feces intermittently which can make diagnosis difficult. It can also go dormant within the body and thus be undetected for long periods. Additionally, it has the ability to quickly develop resistance to conventional drugs. Prevention of transmission to humans is best accomplished by *thoroughly* washing any part of your body that was in contact with a suspected carrier, its infected cage, feces, or any bodily fluids. ***This should be a standard practice after handling any herp!*** A solution of liquid chlorine bleach (e.g. Clorox®) in water, in a ratio of 1 part bleach to 9 parts water, kills *Salmonella* bacteria within ten minutes of constant exposure, as do many other disinfectants such as Roccal-D® and Nolvasan®. Avoid using cleaners containing phenols such as Lysol™ and Pine-Sol™ which are toxic to corn snakes.

SKIN AILMENTS

Corn snakes heal remarkably rapidly from injuries to their integuments (skin). Any surface damage usually accelerates the frequency of shedding to aid in regeneration of skin and scales. The most common types of dermal injuries come from **burns** from unshielded or malfunctioning heating devices. The best way to avoid this is to imagine whether it would be physically possible for your corn snake to press itself against, or wrap itself around, whatever supplemental heating device you're using. If there's a way, they'll figure it out sooner or later and cram themselves into a position that burns them before they can escape. You'd think it were impossible that they could act so 'stupidly', until the day you're faced with treating the "open wound that couldn't happen." Treatment is much more difficult than prevention, so heed this warning. For minor burns, application of a topical antibiotic such as Polysporin Ointment® or Silvadine® Creme daily to the affected areas should be performed until healing occurs. For more severe burns, a qualified reptile veterinarian should be consulted.

Bites from live prey are also familiar to most keepers. Avoiding it should be intuitive, but there will be times occasionally when a live rodent is left in a cage unsupervised over an extended period 'for a good reason.' We personally haven't thought of it yet, but it's an excuse we hear often, so you may confront it someday. Clean such wounds with a water flush, and then apply a broad-spectrum antimicrobial liquid mix comprised of hydrogen peroxide (diluted 50/50 with water) and Betadine® added to achieve the color of weak iced tea. Use immediately and discard remainder. Afterwards, apply an antibiotic such as Neosporin® cream, or one of the Furacin™ creams meant to speed healing in people. For injuries covering areas larger than a square half-inch (1 cm²), a sterile patch can be taped over the area to prevent infection and further abrasion. Place the injured snake in its cage on plain paper temporarily to reduce chances of loose particles of substrate entering the healing wound. Bites from belligerent cagemates or especially ardent suitors during courtship (or unintended male-male combat) rarely are deep or serious. Their care is the same after checking for any broken teeth in the wound.

Blisters and discoloration may crop up between or under scales, especially the ventral plates, if the cage environment stays excessively damp for more than a few days at one time. Increased moisture allows bacteria to grow on feces, old shed skins, organic substrates, and any other nutrients that exist. Skin diseases often appear under the belly scutes first since they have the greatest contact with the floor, although they can occur anywhere on the body. The most frequent cause of persistent dampness is a tipped or overflowing water bowl. Use only heavy bowls with vertical sides or with sides angled inward, which are less prone to tipping. Fill the bowl only halfway to minimize spillage when corn snakes coil up inside. When corns occasionally soak non-stop for many days preparatory to molting, or to rid themselves of mites, the layers of old and new skin or active bite wounds form an ideal protected environment for bacteria to get a foothold. Remove bowls temporarily if you see your snakes in them constantly, offering only tiny drinking basins for awhile instead, and inspect snakes thoroughly for any evidence of problems. Snakes will shed more frequently as part of the recovery process to promote faster healing after such skin problems. Applying Silvadine® cream to injured areas will speed the healing. Serious injuries or excessive blistering may additionally require a herp veterinarian to prescribe a systemic antibiotic to fight infection. Piperacillin® has been known to be very effective in treating blister disease when given at a dosage of 80 mg/kg IM every 72 hours for a period of 30 days.

MOUTHROT

As tame as corn snakes are, they don't like being confined to small shipping cups or sacks or even to cages they deem too restrictive or otherwise unsatisfactory. They explore every nook and cranny for an escape route, sometimes pushing their snouts into each one with impressive force. This, plus random nips by prey animals while being subdued, is a common cause of stomatitis or mouth rot. The mouth lining and gums are quite sensitive to injury because bacterial infections thrive in moist, dark places. Typically a whitish or yellowish substance resembling cheese builds up over an infected area causing swelling, an inability to completely close the mouth, or the formation of a scab. Unlike a scab on a person, however, most opinions favor *carefully* and *gently* removing the scab from a corn, using a cloth or tweezers and treating the infection daily until completely healed. This malady is quite curable, but requires persistence on the keeper's part to maintain the wearisome routine. Mild cases of mouthrot may be treated topically with Listerine® or a hydrogen peroxide and Betadine® solution. (Mix hydrogen peroxide and water 50/50, and add Betadine® until the color of the solution resembles weak iced tea). Apply with a cotton swab to the affected area twice daily. *Note: Do not apply liberal amounts of either liquid in order to avoid ingestion. In more severe cases, a qualified reptile veterinarian should be consulted for a bacterial culture and the appropriate antibiotic. Be aware that stomatitis can lead to infections in the jaw bone, septicemia and death. Treat this condition seriously; delayed or inconsistent treatment could be fatal.

RESPIRATORY DISORDERS

Signs in *Elaphe guttata* include many of the same symptoms of an upper respiratory disease in humans – wheezing, sneezing, mucus coming from the nostrils and mouth, breathing through the mouth instead of the nostrils, lethargy, and maybe even a rattling gurgly feeling from within them when held. It is possible to treat a mild respiratory infection at home by providing a warm, dry environment. Raise the temperature to the high end of the snake's preferred temperature range, around 89-92°F (31.5–33.3°C), the equivalent of giving it an artificial fever to help it fight germs, and eliminate all possible stresses. The sick snake should be isolated in a separate cage, and even a separate room if possible, to avoid spreading the problem. A trip to the veterinarian for a bacterial culture and an antibiotic is recommended for more serious or stubborn cases.

EGG-BINDING (DYSTOCIA)

Occasionally a female corn fails to pass some or all of her clutch of eggs, retaining them far longer than is normal or healthy for her. An egg-binding problem is most noticeable as either an out-of-proportion or irregular bulge in a female's lower abdomen. It may also be felt as a lump or hardened mass in her body about the time you expect her to deposit her clutch, or immediately afterward. We believe that this particular problem is largely a consequence of captivity, although we suspect it *could* happen in nature, too. It may be that she can't find a suitable nest site in her cage when the time comes, in which case certain good mothers delay oviposition hoping to find a better site. At first she'll anxiously explore the cage at odd times until tired, possibly denting in or soiling her nose in her fervent quest. Then she rests while building the strength to try again. The remedy is obvious – put more choices of nest sites in her enclosure that are bigger, darker, moister or drier.

After years of experience and the witnessing of literally thousands of nestings, we feel safe in surmising that a combination of lack of exercise, and less-varied (but abundant) food in captive diets contributes to poorer muscle tone and the inability of females to pass eggs naturally (dystocia). We, like many breeders who went through a commercial phase, kept our corns in cramped boxes, fed them heavily, and tried to prime them for second clutches whenever possible. Years of this regimen allowed us to watch the egg-binding phenomenon become slightly more common each season until a massive move to roomier caging eased its rate of incidence several years ago.

We've also started a policy of offering the first pre-killed rodent of the meal (whenever we use them, which is *not* 100% of the time) from long forceps to fake the struggling of live prey so the snake constricts it upon grabbing it and thus exercises a little. Joe Hiduke informed us that the huge corn snake colony he manages is fed more live prey than thawed frozen, and his perception is that it's a contributing factor in the frequency of dystocias decreasing noticeably. Even periodic handling (when snakes are not gravid or full of food) is a form of exercise that specimens in large collections seldom experience.

When eggs get stuck and it's determined that a female will not be passing them without help, several options exist. (An X-ray from a qualified reptile veterinarian may be warranted at this point to determine position and size). Manual palpation may persuade the egg(s) to move downward. In our experience, they usually won't budge, but it's worth a quick try. *DO NOT* apply any really forceful effort – this is delicate territory! Trying to move an egg from too far anterior to the cloaca can rupture it along the way if it's at all irregular. Or, it may snag along the way and cause a portion of the oviduct to be damaged or prolapse (be expelled out the cloaca). When the egg is within about 3 inches of the cloaca, we've successfully used a slender lubricated probe gently inserted up the cloaca to encircle the egg and loosen it while also relaxing the opening itself. Careful manipulation should then be able to ease the egg out. Make sure that the probe is in contact with the egg, not oviduct membrane, before guiding the egg out so it doesn't pull the oviduct out first.

The next effort is one that we tried experimentally about a decade ago with excellent results. Its object is to deflate the most posterior stuck egg, which we presume is the one causing the problem. Sometimes an exceptionally large, odd-shaped one gets jammed, or one gets infected or dies *in utero* and swells to block the others. Swabbing the skin surface adjacent to the widest point with an alcohol wipe or Betadine®, we then aim for the stretched skin between scales. We puncture the egg from outside the body using an 18-gauge needle on a 10-cc or larger syringe. We're very careful to push the needle in only *half* the estimated diameter so the tip ends up in the approximate center of the egg. If the egg is accessible from the cloacal opening, we enter through that to avoid puncturing the body wall at all. Either way, a second person is necessary to securely hold the snake while this is done. The plunger is slowly withdrawn to aspirate the egg contents, repeating the procedure more than once if necessary, and being very carful not to inject egg yolk into the body cavity during withdrawal. The area is again swabbed to clean it, and the snake is returned to a sterile cage for at least 24 hours.

Far more occasionally than not, the remainder of the clutch is passed by morning, in fully salvageable condition. If it is only partially passed, the procedure may be repeated within a few days on the most posterior of the remaining eggs. If you postpone acting on it for more than a week or so, the egg contents harden and aspiration often becomes impossible. Although an obvious chance for infection exists, we've never encountered it in dozens of such procedures and have gone on to breed those females in later years with good results.

Taking a different tack, an intramuscular injection of oxytocin, a drug used to induce birthing labor in women, stimulates contractions in the oviduct to get the eggs moving. And in a really serious situation when nothing else works and the snake is getting physically weak, true surgery is the only option left to remove an impassable clutch. A veterinarian is best sought for both of these last resort methods. *Important:* within a few days *after* egg deposition, check the female's entire body length carefully by hand to detect potential problems like egg retention. This is the time, when you're distracted by setting up the new clutch of eggs, that smaller, harder bad eggs may be left behind and easily missed by only a casual visual inspection of the mother.

STRESS AND THE UNKNOWN

Stress is still the "black hole" of disorders, but it's starting to catch at least partial blame these days as the cause, or at least precursor, of a multitude of maladies. We all know that nervous snakes don't act normally or feed regularly. Why shouldn't other forms of stress affect different aspects of their behavior too, as it does in humans? The signs are usually less obvious than the straight-forward refusal of food, so it's up to us as their caretakers to observe, access, and react to subtle indications of these problems and contribute new solutions. We certainly don't have all the answers yet, but as concerned herpetoculturists, we are interested in advancing this area of study. A few examples may help illustrate some things we've noticed so far and emphasize the importance of speculating further on this oft-neglected topic.

Our favorite culprit is the syndrome of captivity that could be dubbed 'limited freedom of choice.' It ends up working its way into a large percentage of the answers we give to people by phone and in print. Simply summed up, *most* captive situations (we're including the bulging ranks of new people keeping corn snakes in our assessment of *most*) do not offer the voluntary range of daily environmental choices available in the wild. Snakes can't warm up or cool down quickly by moving in or out of the sun to change body temperature. This severely affects their natural ability to digest food optimally, to hamper diseases or parasites by exposing them to extremes (like when *our* bodies create fever conditions), or to regulate other hormonal functions which we haven't yet investigated. Their choice of wetness or dryness (we mean ambient conditions, not merely having drinking water available or not) may aid in shedding cleanly or curing fungal infections. Having a truly safe retreat for those times when snakes prefer to shut down all activity levels and avoid disturbance (while digesting a prodigious meal, while in shed, at egg deposition time, etc.) may be more necessary than we suspect. Complex hormonal functions may require total relaxation and privacy to proceed in an orderly fashion for the next phase of their bodies' physiological needs. Even the vibrations bouncing through an active household, and ultimately their cages, may leave snakes in a constant state of minor agitation because it's a non-ignorable instinct to take heed of such signals as potential danger.

Our love of convenience often dictates offering a monotonously unvarying diet of domestic rodents to our charges. Is it unreasonable to think that wild corns sometimes take to the trees to specifically seek avian prey for a change of pace, analogous to the cravings of pregnant women for unusual foods? Maybe corns even occasionally revert to their youthful diet of frogs or lizards when their bodies tell them to seek a needed dose of vitamins or minerals they lack. In captivity they also lose whatever benefit they may derive from trace minerals ingested in the guts of natural wild prey. Can this be of greater long-term significance than anyone currently suspects?

The quality of our heavily treated city water supplies may be slowly poisoning our snakes with an accumulation of trace elements that they, as small-bodied organisms, have lower tolerances for than humans. Cage water also tends to sit for long spells, weeks if we use conveniently oversize bowls that don't empty quickly, creating a stagnant pool in which pathogens can multiply, protected from sun, rain, and wind that would normally sterilize, dilute, or dry up a water source.

Possibly an even more commonplace offense is our controlling the timing of light our animals live under to suit our whim. Who isn't guilty of casually flipping on the lights at some odd hour to check something, or worse yet, to pull the snake out from cover to show a visitor? What would *your* reaction to such an intrusion be at 3:00 AM when you were sound asleep? Since we know that most animals and plants are still far more closely linked than people to the natural photoperiods that govern their life cycles, such disruptions could critically affect the fine-tuning of the biological clocks they may depend upon for normal daily life.

The quality of light may also be an important factor we've thus far dismissed of significance. We know from human tests that the effects of nonnatural tones of light, as are emitted by most incandescent and fluorescent bulbs, affect peoples' moods and productivity. We already know that ultraviolet components of sunlight are essential for some other herp species to properly metabolize elements of their diets. For species so heavily influenced by the one and only source of light that forever dominates their lives, the sun, is it unreasonable to assume that altering its intensity or wavelength spectrum will have some effect?

Murkier realms exist. Pollution from agricultural and industrial chemicals, hormones, and poisons have created a worrisome new area of scientific concern – endocrine disruption. Complicated biological processes like embryonic development are being distorted by exposure to even traces of them entering the environment. Altering just one link in the precise chain of events in an organism's growth can spell doom. What could ultrasonic communications frequencies that now reverberate across our planet be doing to unknown snake senses needed in migration, finding mates, evaluating changing weather, etc? Could we be short-circuiting the finely tuned sensory systems of many lower lifeforms without even being conscious of the disruption because our own limited senses are (apparently) not affected adversely? We present these thoughts to inspire deeper examination of the complexities of life and how we may be unwittingly affecting them for our captives and ourselves.

PART IV - COLOR AND PATTERN VARIATION

COLOR & PATTERN

Showy colors first attract most people to corn snakes as pets. Then the realization of the myriad variations they can display hits home, and that anyone can easily manipulate these traits in successive captive generations. It's like the latent artist in us all finding a new format to explore, using a canvas that already fascinates us. And if intrinsic beauty isn't enough to entice us, the prospect of monetary reward from breeding success looms on a not-too-distant horizon.

The naturally occurring races of *Elaphe guttata* were covered briefly in the introduction. What wasn't really elaborated upon was the tremendous range of natural color variation within particular subspecies and even between individuals of local populations. No photo, or even dozens of them, can completely prepare you for what the next specimen may look like. This point is often missed by inexperienced individuals trying to key out species in a field guide that emphasizes picture identifications. It also causes misunderstandings when people have the tendency to lock onto a favorite image of a nice-looking corn in a book or magazine. People forget about variation and the fact that photographers are strongly motivated to shoot the most attractive subjects possible in order to sell their photos. Hobbyists expect to be able to obtain a snake just like the picture by simply ordering one sporting the same label on a pricelist, assuming it will be exactly the same.

Spending a day people-watching at the mall will make this lesson obvious as you try to think of a way to describe the average human being. Or, if you've ever rated members of the opposite sex on a scale of 1 to 10, you know the range of differences is undeniable and often a source of great interest or desire. The analogy translates well to corn snakes. All field guides showing corn snakes face the so far insurmountable dilemma of depicting what's in the wild with the limited number of photos that can be allowed to represent each species. Since no two corns look exactly alike, your experience will forever be limited to the chosen few that end up in print and to the ones you're able to see alive. Don't despair - this is good and exciting news! It means that the *guttata* universe is still expanding, and there's plenty of room for everyone to participate in its continuing cultivation and evolution. In this chapter we'll discuss all known color and pattern traits in corns. To paint a backdrop before delving into them and the genetics of variations, we'll first examine the naturally occurring corn snake morphs that are frequently seen today.

NATURALLY-OCCURRING CORN MORPHS

Average *Elaphe guttata* have a row of 30-50 large squarish or rectangular blotches running down the midline of their backs. The first one is usually connected to a spearhead-shaped marking atop the head, and the last one is virtually at the tail's tip. A second set of smaller and more irregularly shaped markings alternate with the dorsal blotches along the sides, although the lateral blotches vary tremendously in size, shape, and exact placement. All these blotches have black or dark outlines of varying thicknesses and centers of some shade of red, orange, brown, or some combination of them. The ground color between blotches may be any shade of yellow to orangish red, or lean toward a light to dark grey or tan. The wide belly scales (ventral scutes) may be white, yellow, red or orange, and are usually marked with a series of roughly geometrical shapes in contrasting black. All these traits are subject to alteration over relatively short periods of time (one to three years per generation on average) through selective breeding, which is one reason why corns are such popular study species for ongoing herpetocultural projects.

'OKEETEE' CORNS

This is the quintessentially ultimate yet normal corn snake, encompassing all the traits that people love in the species as a whole. Carl Kauffeld popularized this big, husky 'race' in two books about snake hunting - Snakes and Snake Hunting, 1957 and Snakes - The Keeper and the Kept, 1969. The name was bestowed in honor of the property on which they were first collected – the Okeetee Hunt Club. Not only has 'Okeetee' withstood the test of time, it has become the general designation for classically beautiful corns from the southern tip of South Carolina. Collectors have since descended upon the region annually, especially in the spring, to experience the thrill of field collecting that renowned hot spot for ultra gorgeous corn snakes.

'Okeetee' corn snakes include, but are not limited to, individuals with deep red dorsal blotches ringed by well-defined, jet-black borders. The ground color ranges from russet to bright orange and is contrasted clearly and cleanly by the distinctive black. Two dorsal and two lateral hazy dark stripes, more prominent on some individuals than others, may appear over the blotches for the length of the body. The belly tends to be mostly plain white for most of its length, with a prominent squarish black checkerboard pattern covering it for approximately half its surface area. The posterior ventrals may also have some orange between the checkering.

It is now known that attractive corns fitting this general description inhabit the entire Atlantic Coastal Plain from eastern North Carolina down into northeastern Florida. More importantly, and often neglected in the fervor to find the most exquisite example, not every animal from the Okeetee region will be a classic beauty. Some will be very ordinary in looks, and a few will be rather dull and unremarkable. However, after years of selective breeding, typical captive

Not all corns are ravishing beauties! This is a completely average-looking specimen collected in lower southeastern Florida. Note the "dirty wash" of melanin muddying the colors, and the four faint dark stripes that are common on many corns living in the wild. These stripes alone are not evidence that they are hybrids with yellow rat snakes.

Hatchling corns have yet to develop their normal complement of yellow that later provides their beautiful range of orange tones. The two 'Okeetee' corns shown are full siblings one year apart in age.

Specimens from the Okeetee region of southern South Carolina have long been hailed as the quintessential beauties of the corn snake world. Bold black and white ventral patterns are one of their trademark features along with bright, high-contrast dorsal coloration.

Collectors have also bred to preserve the thick black borders on 'Okeetee' corns that help delineate blotches from ground colors.

'Okeetee'corns are often stunningly colored compared to average specimens of *guttata*. This fact has unfortunately been exploited occasionally to help sell normal, undifferentiated hatchlings, or offspring "diluted" from 'Okeetee' stock crossed to something else, since the Okeetee name has become synonymous with the stunning coloration many collectors seek. It's also a feature that isn't easily judged in very young examples.

'MIAMI PHASE'

The name for this morph is derived from specimens commonly found in the agricultural areas south and west of Miami, Florida, around which *E. guttata* occurs in incredibly high densities. They typically display a silvery-grey background color with various amounts of orange dusting or speckling mixed into it, although not all examples adhere very closely to "the standard" we've described. The dorsal blotch color is generally more orange than red, often with whitish spots or pale centers, especially towards the sides. At its best, with the ground color and dorsal blotches appearing as pure, even tones, this morph resembles a light phase gray-banded king snake (*Lampropeltis alterna*). In reality, most snakes exhibit flaws in the smoothness or uniformity of the grey and orange. Hatchlings from this area often tend to average a little smaller size than other strains of corns, and a small but significant percentage prefer lizards, especially *Anolis* lizards, to pink mice for their first meals. Once started, they are no different than any other corn. Adults can grow as large as more northern corns, but Miami phase corns are often smaller, averaging only three to four feet (91-122 cm) in length.

Rich Zuchowski is developing a variant dubbed '**Milk snake phase.**' It is essentially an enhanced '**Miami phase**' corn in which some examples exhibit very uniform blotching on a clean grayish-white background. Their resemblance to certain cleanly patterned milk snakes, like *Lampropeltis triangulum temporalis* from the Atlantic coastal plain of the northeastern U.S., formed the basis of the name for this intensified version of an old favorite.

From the preceding accounts, it should be plain that any variation could become the next "new" captive morph with some selective breeding effort. It merely takes somebody to notice a standout specimen, with unusual or appealing traits that might be reliably reproduced and preferably accentuated or even exaggerated. Since there are no official rules about naming color or pattern variants, as exist in scientific circles when describing species, new names have only to stand the "market test" for a few years to determine if their creation is distinct in the eyes of the public. Ultimately, a second trait - long-term desirability – will decide if a variant can withstand the test of time. If it does, it will remain available as a recognized morph that hobbyists and breeders preserve through captive breeding. With snakes, we've coined this phenomenon "passing the hatband test," referencing both the usage of snake skins as decorations on cowboy hats and comparing it to the potential lasting power of clothes fashions, which depend on the breadth and endurance of their visual appeal.

GENETICS

B-o-r-i-n-g! You may be tempted to think *"I'd better move on to the pictures because this is bound to be complicated. Besides, I can always call the breeder and ask what I'll get if I cross a green-blotched snow-stripe with a ghost motley het for albinism... ."* We're acutely aware of the difficulty people have with this subject, and are trying to make it as simple as possible in the section that follows. Mainly we'll concentrate on *what* happens, especially regarding simple dominant vs. recessive genetics, and let you proceed to an academic biology text for most of the fine details of the *hows* and *whys* of the more complex stuff. Also, check out this book's appendix for getting a free computer program that will help take much of the guesswork out of predicting hatch ratios of most forms of recessive color and pattern mutations in corn snakes.

Many popular corn snake color variations are *not* merely normal or extra nice versions of morphs currently found in nature. They appeared when a recessive gene was paired with another copy of itself in a single snake and that snake fell into a breeder's hands. Amelanistic ("regular albinism") is the classic example; it was the first and multiplied geometrically to propel herpetoculture and corn snakes to where they are today.

Odd new recessive traits are showing up with much greater frequency than just a decade or two ago, for two good reasons. With the booming popularity of herp keeping, more people are in the field catching wild herps for the pet trade. Not only are more corn snakes being caught, more gravid females are collected proportionately, dropping their eggs to hatch in captivity. Spurred by the contemporary widespread employment of captive breeding techniques to proliferate traits that please us, those hunters are keeping an extra sharp eye peeled for any individuals, caught by or hatching for them, that sport a slightly different look. They know that people are ready and willing to pay a premium price for the chance to work with something new, especially if it may net them future profits.

New genes often alter animals so that they are not as fit for survival in the wild as the normal looking types. Abnormally colored specimens may be easier for predators to find and eat, like amelanistics which do not blend into the natural background, but rather "glow" against it. And maybe the amelanistics' lack of pigmentation makes them vulnerable to harmful solar rays. These individuals usually perish as juveniles without ever being seen by humans.

The second reason for an increased frequency of recessive traits is the nature of recessive genes. In corn snakes, as in humans, genes exercise their control over phenotypes (appearances) in pairs, with one of each pair received from each parent. If both parents contribute a normal gene for a trait, then the baby shows the normal trait. If one parent passes a normal gene, and a recessive abnormal gene is inherited from the other parent (such as one of the pair needed to cause the lack of

A high percentage of corns from extreme southeastern Florida have red-orange blotches on gray backgrounds, giving them a rather distinctive appearance. Not every specimen conforms to the 'Miami phase' corn standard, however, and the gray ground color shows up in individuals from many other scattered localities too.

The 'Milk snake phase' corn's larger blotches and pale ground color cause it to superficially resemble certain milk snakes from the Atlantic Coastal Plain in the northeastern U.S. *Photo by Rich Zuchowski*

The elimination of all white flecks, leaving only reds and oranges, is the goal when breeding 'Sunglow' amelanistic corns.

Albino 'Okeetec' corns look like amelanistic versions of normal 'Okeetee' corns in which the black blotch rings are reversed to white.

black pigment in corns), then the babies still show the normal trait. The single recessive gene is masked by the dominant gene for black which alone can oversee the normal production of that pigment. Babies carrying the genes for, but not showing such a recessive trait, are *heterozygous*, which literally means having a pair of non-identical genes, or mixed genetic heritage, concerning a particular trait. It is the opposite of *homozygous*, the state in which both genes governing a single trait are identical. The term heterozygous is often shortened to 'hetero', or just 'het' on dealers' and breeders' pricelists.

When recessive genes result in a different, non-normal appearance in a corn snake, such as amelanism, it's because those genes are existing in a paired homozygous state. If even one of the gene pair is for the normal (dominant) look with black pigment, it dominates the trait and negates any influence of the recessive gene. Recessive genes *must* be in a homozygous state to exert their effect.

Recessive genes are more likely to get paired in small groups of animals, like captive colonies in which related individuals breed together and share gene pools, than in large populations of unrelated ones that have 'strangers' carrying fresh genes moving in and out haphazardly. Animals in a collection, especially after a couple generations of successful matings (and holding back of future breeding stock from the offspring produced), tend to share much more genetic material than any random group of specimens in the field. Consequently, new traits pop up relatively more often in captivity than in free-roaming wild populations. When it happens in nature, the new mutation offers the population a potential boost that might let it take advantage of new conditions and prove to be beneficial in the long run. If it doesn't improve survival chances, and most of the fancy traits we admire do not, few individuals are wasted in "the experiment," and those showing the trait die off before getting old enough to pass on their genes.

Many aspiring breeders have been warned to avoid inbreeding their captive herps if possible, but they don't really know why. The simplest explanation is that inbreeding (mating animals closely related to one another in their family ancestry) concentrates traits, good and bad, within family lines. This increases the likelihood that undesirable traits will show up after two carriers of those genes mate. Hidden recessive traits probably exist in many individuals, lurking in a heterozygous state. They'll tend to get paired with similar recessive genes in other corns and be able to show themselves sooner when more potential mates in the vicinity also carry the gene. Traits that would be disadvantageous in the wild, such as the many mutations in corn snakes that affect skin colors and patterns, are harmless and even desirable in the safety of captivity. But undesirable traits also show up, such as kinked spines or deformed scales or eyes. Breeders must select their stock carefully, culling out animals with physical deformities and breeding only those specimens exhibiting solely the desirable and non-harmful traits.

The mixing of various color and pattern traits has become a favorite pastime among hobbyists. Fortunately this combats inbreeding depression – the tendency for inbred strains to weaken over time due to a build-up of undesirable recessive genes. Common effects of this syndrome are shorter than normal body lengths, lower weights, eye defects, lower egg and clutch sizes, skeletal imperfections, and infertility. Crossing unrelated corns to bring new traits in also refreshes all the "hidden" recessive genes that were accumulating after successive generations of inbreeding efforts. This process, the phenomenon of hybrid vigor, is common, even essential, in the wild to maintain healthy populations. In nature, it is accomplished through the long-range wanderings of male corn snakes as they seek mates further afield in spring.

At the same time, we also mustn't rule out the possibility that bizarre physical anomalies, resembling the bubble-eyes of goldfish, or the flat, pushed-in faces of Persian cats, may purposely be striven for in the not-so-distant future. A hatchling corn showing such an aberration might be dismissed as undesirable by 99% of us and immediately destroyed, but it takes only one person to nurture such a mutant and perpetuate its characteristics while turning the gross defect into a unique selling point. Exactly this kind of situation currently exists in the line of pure white (**leucistic**) Texas rat snakes *Elaphe obsoleta lindheimeri*, some of which inherit a bug-eyed enlargement of the eyes. Most people consider it an ugly negative attribute to be avoided, while a few people believe that it does the snakes no harm and are working to accentuate the trait over future generations.

What's on the herpetocultural horizon- a race of bicephalic corns?

This hatchling amelanistic Great Plains rat *Elaphe guttata emoryi* cropped up recently in Kansas to introduce a new genetic form of amelanism to corn snakes. *Photo by Brent Ward.*

'Candycane' amelanistic corns are bred to resemble their namesakes with only bright blotches against as pure a white ground color as possible. Outcrossing to other races of *guttata* that mostly lack yellow and red between their dorsal saddles is one way to try to amplify the contrast over future generations.

'Creamsicle' amelanistic corns borrowed a Great Plains rat snake in their genetic background to bring out the yellows when crossed into standard amelanistic corns from the southeastern U.S.

As an adult, an amelanistic *E. g. emoryi* exhibits strong yellow tones that are masked effectively by the darker browns and grays of typically colored specimens. Photo by Don Soderberg and Ryan Moss

GENETIC COLOR MUTATIONS

AMELANISM

Also known as '**albino**', or '**red albino**', the proper name for this trait is *amelanistic*, meaning without black pigment. The main confusion in these terms arises from the fact that the word 'albino' is derived from the Latin word, *albus*, meaning white. It was originally applied to the condition in humans where melanin, our only pigment, was absent. This mutation is one of the most commonly occurring in nature in all kinds of vertebrate animals, but the old assumption that it results in a white animal, as it does in mammals, doesn't apply to reptiles with their several different skin pigments. Corn snakes also have red and yellow pigments, and a layer of cells in their skins called iridophores, or "reflective cells", that are responsible for the whites, prismatic luster, and other subtle tones of the other colors. Taking black away from corn snakes leaves plenty of dazzling color, which often appears brighter than normal without the overcoating of melanin. The multitude of colors complicates the genetics but allows a much greater array of color combinations to occur when mixing and matching genes. Neonates' yellow pigmentation develops during the first several months after hatching, further muddying the immediate prediction of adult coloration. Take heart - those dark reddish-brown babies will improve steadily and quickly.

Amelanism has become common in herpetoculture thanks to the efforts of Dr. H. Bernard Bechtel of Valdosta, Georgia. He obtained a wild-caught male amelanistic corn, collected in North Carolina back in 1953, and used it to breed three normal females in 1959. The offspring all appeared normal in coloration, but were heterozygous for amelanism. This exemplifies a basic rule of genetics when dealing with simple recessive genes, as most of the color mutations in corns have proven to be: *If at least one parent of a pair is actually displaying a mutation, all of their first generation offspring will carry the gene (be heterozygous for it).*

When Dr. Bechtel mated these first filial generation (F1) heterozygous offspring together two years later, the recessive amelanistic genes were brought back together again in a predictable ratio. According to the laws of genetics, one quarter of the second generation (F2) offspring would end up receiving two genes for amelanism, one from each F1 heterozygous parent, and thus would be homozygous for stopping black pigment production. Approximately one quarter of the clutch from each of the three females did indeed hatch as amelanistic corns, proving amelanism to be a simple recessive trait as suspected.

Those laws also say that another quarter of the F2 offspring would be completely normal in appearance and homozygous in their genealogy (genetic make-up). The rest of the babies – approximately half of the litter -would look normal too but be gene-carriers (hets) for amelanism like their F1 parents. It would not be possible to distinguish which of the normal-looking corns that made up three quarters of the total F2 hatchlings were carrying the recessive gene for amelanism until they in turn were raised and bred, and their F3 generation of offspring hatched to reveal their colorations.

Although first reproduced in captivity in 1961, the strain wasn't widely available or well known until the early 1970s after recipients of donated specimens from Dr. Bechtel eventually made their own surplus captive-bred progeny available to the public. A few people, who had heard about but not actually seen them yet, were a little confused and disappointed to find out that the animals were not white, but instead were red, orange, and yellow with pink eyes. The brilliant hatchlings delighted the newly emerging herp hobbyist sector when they first were offered for sale in the $300-$500 range each! The price was high, especially at the time, but it was eagerly paid due to two big advantage dangled in front of prospective buyers' noses: *1) they were easily breedable, and 2) there was no competition from amelanistic snakes captured in the wild.* The initial expense could be recouped from sales of captive-bred offspring. Early propagation and financial successes with 'albino' corn snakes launched the modern herpetocultural era of the past three decades!

It's significant to note that yellow, being a late rising pigment, does not hold true in a very new phase of the western subspecies *L. g. emoryi* developed by Don Soderberg. His new 'albino' race has pure yellow blotches on pale pinkish white at hatching, and retains the look throughout life. It's also definitely *not* the same gene, proven through two years of breeding crosses, that causes the same genetic loss of black that's shared by all the other amelanistic corns around today. This new form finally gives us two bloodlines in *Elaphe guttata* that lack the pigment melanin, just as has existed in the black rat snake, *Elaphe o. obsoleta,* for decades.

SPECIAL VARIETIES OF AMELANISTIC CORNS

The various shades of red, yellow, black and white combine in a multitude of ways, depending on the appearance of the original normal ancestors. Particularly significant is how prevalent each color was in them, and exactly where it was distributed over their bodies. In the early to mid 1980s, herpetoculturists started to focus on more than just indiscriminately breeding more amelanistic corns. We, and a couple other people, began to selectively breed specimens that already showed some promise of extreme or unusual coloration, much as has been done with the normal corns discussed earlier. One of the most popular strains today exhibits smooth red/orange blotches on a clean orange background with very little or no white speckling. The earliest animals we obtained in our own work on this variation trace back to Norm Damm in Ohio, and ultimately to Vince Scheidt in California. Over several more generations, we and other breeders were able to select the characteristics to obtain the consistent colors seen in most of today's specimens.

The 'Fluorescent orange' morph of amelanistic corns concentrates on the brilliance of the red-orange background color and wide white blotch borders to make it stand out in a crowd. *Photo by Rich Zuchowski*

Amelanistic corns are the most popular pet snake in the world! Note that they are mainly only red and white until the yellows develop over many months.

Type A anerythristic corns lack all red pigmentation, and most yellow too. Although it has shown up in far-flung locations within the range of *Elaphe g. guttata*, it's relatively common in portions of southwestern Florida in the wild.

The 'Charcoal' corn is anerythristic, but it further lacks even the hints of yellow on the chin of type As. Young specimens, especially neonates, also have a faint bluish glare on the scales of the head.

We originally called his morph "no-white albino", but changed it later to the more memorable (and saleable) '**Sunglow**.' Our coining of that non-normal cultivar in *Elaphe guttata* helped set off a trend that has flourished. It has propelled widespread adoption of the practice as thousands of private herpetoculturists now participate in similar selective breeding projects and the subsequent marketing of the progeny. Various efforts are underway to intensify the red aspect with the addition of bloodred corn bloodlines that should eventually fuse those traits into one incredibly brilliant red corn snake morph. Others are attempting to breed the 'no-white' color coverage into primarily yellow '**Creamsicle**' and '**Butter**' corns, with the goal of achieving a real dazzler with deep red blotches on a glowing yellow background.

During the mid-late 1980s, we noticed that a few specimens in our colony possessed unusually large white borders around the blotches and singled them out for a special project. One particular beauty from Mike & Linda Krick had a special flare towards that trait. As more offspring accumulated in our colony, we remarked how some of those attractive animals were reminiscent of classic Okeetee corns, only with white replacing the usual black outlining of the blotches. They still provided the same pleasing contrast, with even more brilliant colors because of the lack of black. The ground color was distinctly lighter yellowish-orange than the blotch tone, which provided additional contrast. Naturally, we started looking for and selectively breeding for this trait, especially trying to breed for ever-wider white rings. Subsequently other corns were crossed in when they exhibited some characteristic that might heighten the effect. It was *not* necessary that all were descended from Okeetee stock since the emphasis was on appearance, not heritage. They became known first as the 'reverse Okeetee', later as the '**Albino Okeetee**' corn snake, based on looks alone.

Concurrently, Glen Slemmer of Vancouver, British Columbia, was crossing Great Plains rats *(E. g. emoryi)* with amelanistic corns to increase the amount of yellow pigment and to decrease the red, hoping to create a golden yellow-orange variation of corn. The resulting subspecific crosses can range from golden yellow to, more often, an orangish butterscotch color. The one constant is that they lack any real red. True to its *emoryi* roots, clutch sizes tend to be smaller than those found for pure corns, but the babies are often larger and more robust and easy to get started feeding on newborn mice. The name '**Creamsicle**' was coined along the way, presumably due to its pastel orange resemblance to a popular frozen dessert on a stick. That silly-sounding moniker may be one of the reasons it has become a well-remembered favorite to this day in the pet trade.

Interestingly, the goal of the creamsicle project has been realized in a different way - the **amelanistic Emory's rat snake** – a new strain pioneered by Don Soderberg and only reproduced for the first time in the late 1990s (as discussed earlier in the AMELANISTIC section). We predict that it will soon be crossed and mixed thoroughly with other lines of eastern *guttata* to display all sorts of new color combinations of yellow and red in a vast replay of the aims of the original 'creamsicle' project, and beyond.

'**Candycanes**' are a fourth cultivar of the amelanistic corn that ideally results in a whitish snake with bright red-orange blotches. They were developed by Glen Slemmer, and later named and refined by Kevin Enge, by crossing selected adults with little background color between the dorsal blotches. '**Miami phase**' corn bloodlines with clean light grey areas between the blotches contributed some of the original stock, as did some *E. g. emoryi* with pale backgrounds, '**Creamsicles**' and other amelanistics in other peoples' efforts to perfect them. This color phase has proven to be difficult to produce reliably, still needing a few more generations of selective breeding to produce consistent results.

Because corns gain yellow pigment as they age, babies of all strains often appear very "candycanish", but later blossom out with yellows and oranges in the ground color. Therefore, it is extremely difficult to predict which babies will show the most highly contrasting whitish backgrounds as adults. In refining the candycane strain, serious breeders always hold on to many more babies than they really want for at least six to twelve months to determine which to keep permanently. It's the only reliable way to improve breeding colonies whose ultimate appearance is a product of slow individual changes during maturation. Keep this fact in mind when purchasing hatchlings of this and other strains; even the breeders can't always pick the very best ones at extremely early ages when developing yellow plays a key role in adult appearance.

A fifth variant has been named '**Fluorescent orange.**' It originated with a pair of sibling amelanistic snakes, the female of which Rich Zuchowski felt showed a hint of piebaldism [see later account under CALICO (PIEBALDISM)] when it hatched unexpectedly in 1987. They strongly resemble bright albino Okeetee corns in many ways. Random white splotching has not yet reappeared in subsequent offspring, but the white bordering the dorsal blotches is extra wide and bold, and the ground color between the blotches stands out as an unusually vibrant orange.

ANERYTHRISM

Also known confusingly as '**melanistics**' and '**black albinos**', anerythristic corn snakes possess a recessive genetic defect that leaves them unable to form red and most yellow pigment, similar to the way amelanistics lack black. Superficially they resemble the grey rat snake *Elaphe obsoleta spiloides* or Emory's rat snakes, or a black and white or sepia-tone picture of a typical corn snake. Grays, browns, and blacks predominate in an otherwise normal pattern of blotches. No other color is evident except traces of yellow on the lower throat, chin, and labial areas which may be formed by a separate accumulation of *carotenoids* (red and yellow pigments often contained in natural foods).

This 'Chocolate' Great Plains rat is as close as we've seen to true melanism in *Elaphe guttata*. Its nearly total coverage of melanin and split dorsal blotching may not seem attractive at first glance, but its genetic heritage in both traits might hold keys to new and interesting things when used to mix and match with other variants. Photo by Don Soderberg and Ryan Moss

The bronzing or fading of the black in this corn's saddle rings and ventral checkerboarding clearly show the effects of hypomelanism.

Yellow is more pronounced underlying the blotches and background of a 'Caramel' corn snake than a normally pigmented one. *Photo by Tim Rainwater*

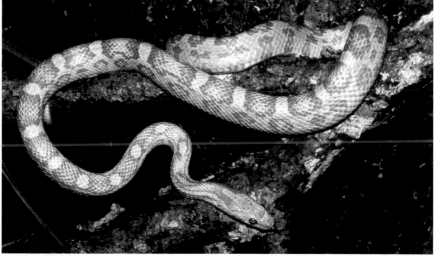

'Lavender' is the very appropriate name that describes this morph in which the entire snake takes on a light purplish cast, and sometimes glowing pink eyes too.

It's also possible that the residual yellow may develop as an actual bodily function that produces yellow pigment by a secondary or back-up system. Maybe it's *only* supposed to add an extra touch of yellow on the throat and labials for reasons we haven't yet determined, and still does so even when it's the only yellow-producing system working at the time. Either of these might also be explanations for the tendency in *some* big anerythristics to fade into a dull brownish with advanced age. Many older snakes take on very meager amounts of reds and/or yellows that muddy the higher contrast black on white of their youths. There must be a mechanism, such as gradual gain through dietary sources, which installs normal corn snake pigments in these older individuals. This means there may be more than one way to achieve the creation of pigments when the primary systems are cancelled genetically by the recessive mutations we've all gotten used to regarding as 'all or nothing traits.'

The anerythristic mutation, sometimes called '**type A anerythrism**', has turned up many times in wild populations. It's not uncommon to find one adorning the road at dusk in the "Immokalee Triangle", an area roughly between Immokalee, Ft. Myers, and Moore Haven in southwestern Florida. Local people see them often enough to call them grey rat snakes, which do not naturally occur that far south. The deficit of red hasn't seemed to unduly burden their chances at survival because they appear to be getting more common. It's not clear yet if this trend may be falsely enhanced by more snake hunters collecting from the region in recent decades. The vast majority of wild-caught specimens from southwest Florida that lack red pigment are the common type A anerythrism. This type helped create virtually all the other morphs that lack red and yellow pigment, including 'snow' corns and 'ghost' corns.

A '**Stonewashed**' morph of anerythrism has emerged that has a faded appearance that mimics the effect of new denim jeans laundered with smooth stones to achieve a weathered look. There may additionally be a second subtle color or pattern-related gene influencing this look, or it may just be a variation in normal anerythrism that hasn't been widely seen or appreciated yet. (* See the brief discussion of what may be a related strain, '**Frosted corns**', further on.)

Having one form of anerythrism that was inherited in the standard recessive manner left it relatively easy to predict offspring from matings involving this trait for years. Then we stumbled upon a second kind of anerythrism in 1984 when we purchased an unusual-looking 2-foot long female that reputedly came from Pine Island, just off the coast of Lee County, Florida. She lacked the yellow found in the neck area of other specimens, and the basic color was a silvery-grey, lacking the usual brownish/yellowish cast. It was not a very flashy or astounding difference, but we noticed it because we were actively seeking anything new in the dealers' shops during those years.

When she produced both anerythristics AND normals when bred to corns of the 'type A anerythrism' and 'snow', we felt that we had discovered some kind of new gene. Normal colored offspring should not have been possible if our Pine Island female's anerythrism had been the same as the type A anerythrism of the male that bred her. Two parent corns exhibiting the same recessive trait (assuming that they aren't both also heterozygous for other traits) are only supposed to be able to give rise to more of the same. After a few more later breedings, we finally concluded that she not only exhibited a new gene - **type B anerythrism**: she was also a carrier for the more common type A as well. The newer strain was previously called '**Muted**', but the designation of '**Charcoal**' has gained favor and replaced it as the accepted cultivar or trade name. Hatchlings are unique in having a faint bluish cast to the eyes and head scales that sets them apart from type A anerythristics in the litter.

Variation exists among 'black albinos' as within all corn morphs, making some contrast highly when endowed with well-differentiated black blotches and pale grayish-white ground colors. We've seen some very dark specimens overall, but none so uniformly black as to be deemed melanistic (a condition in which melanin dominates the appearance, covering a larger than normal percentage of the body). In theory, a truly melanistic corn should strongly resemble a black rat snake (*Elaphe o. obsoleta*) or black racer (*Coluber constrictor*). Something leaning well in the melanistic direction was found in Kansas a few years ago and has been dubbed '**Chocolate**' Emory's by Don Soderberg. He has already proven its heavy brown overwash to be genetically recessive, and will soon be mixing and matching it to explore the possibilities with other morphs.

HYPOMELANISM

So far we've discussed all-or-nothing traits like amelanism in which either the color is present, or it is not. The amount of melanin in corns is also influenced by genes that are responsible for the amount of dirty overwash and the solidity and density of black in all parts of the pattern. The normal tendency is for great variation to exist in these traits among natural populations of corns, such as those in the lower Florida Keys which are generally light-colored with ill-defined blotch borders. Melanin also increases with age in corns, which is why larger older specimens tend to get uglier (darker) than when they were in their primes at about 2 feet (61 cm) long. Even between siblings though, the range of black in evidence can be startling. Any corn having reduced melanin compared to the last one you saw could be described as *hypomelanistic*. This is not what we're talking about when we discuss hypomelanism below.

As the emerging herpetocultural hobby grew, people started looking carefully for other mutations that might add to the palette of colors and patterns that could be manipulated through selective breeding. One simple recessive trait that has shown up in corns as well as other species is the genetically recessive partial reduction of black pigment – hypomelanism as we'll refer to it from this point on. We first became aware of it in the mid 1980s from an animal displayed at George Van

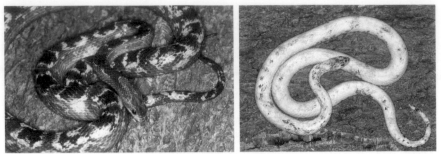

'Calico' corns are an up-and-coming trait that is still under development. This strain starts out looking normal but loses variable amounts of color, which is replaced by white, over random areas of its body as it ages. *Both photos by Tim Rainwater*

Hot on the near herpetocultural horizon is the 'Ruby freckled' corn. Under its influence, 'Snow' corns, the morph it has appeared in first, have slowly gained indiscriminately spaced red splotches with age. *Photo by Bill Love courtesy of Bill Brant & Joe Hiduke*

The 'Motley' trait is barely noticeable in this corn whose blotches are elongated and leaning toward connecting to one another.

'Motley' corns typically have "stretched" dorsal saddles with the tendency to connect strongest closer to the head. This color variant is called the 'Pastel Motley'.

Horn's Reptile World in St. Cloud, Florida. We obtained offspring and eventually reproduced it ourselves through the same strategy as was described for amelanism. Jack Cole also stumbled onto a strain of it from the Tampa, Florida region and was experimenting with it at the same time. Our efforts joined forces soon afterward through the exchanging of specimens.

Although the eyes retain some pigment, they are lighter than the eyes of normal corns but remain darker than the pink eyes of amelanistic corns. The distribution of black pigment is reduced both dorsally and ventrally over the rest of the body. The intensity of the remaining melanin itself is lessened differentially across individuals, often turning black areas anywhere from a chocolate brown or bronze tone to making them fade away almost completely. The difference is best appreciated under bright natural light that allows the quality of the black areas to be judged more accurately than under artificial light. The degree of black reduction in turn affects the brilliance of the underlying colors, leading some breeders to coin the name '**ultra hypos**' to call attention to the instances when extreme fading of melanin coincides with intensely bright base colors.

Hypomelanistic (a.k.a. '**hypo**' and '**rosy**') corns can be at least as attractive as amelanistics because the remaining dark color provides interesting contrast to the cleaned-up, often intense, reds and yellows. As hatchlings they are easily distinguished from normal corns in the same clutch by their overall brighter look. The strain we've bred for more than a decade is clearly inherited as a simple recessive trait, although natural variation still exerts itself on each individual to make the range of differences virtually as great as among normal corns.

Hypomelanism is probably the most under-appreciated and as yet under-utilized recessive trait currently known in *Elaphe guttata*. This won't remain the case for long though because breeders are rushing to explore its "brightening" potential. Don Soderberg has created a spectacular variant on the basic '**Miami phase**' theme by introducing the hypomelanistic gene to make what he calls the '**Hypo Miami**'. Hypomelanism may also be at the root of the odd effect seen on '**Frosted corns**' (see discussion at end of this section). We also suspect that hypoxanthism, in which the normal reds and/or yellows are reduced but not totally eliminated, probably exists already and just hasn't been recognized as such yet; it actually already describes '**Charcoal**' quite accurately. Collectors are now looking for such less obvious anomalies with greater interest as the idea of selective breeding is more widely understood and used to create the astounding number of new cultivars showing up each year.

'CARAMEL'

This morph is the creation of Rich Zuchowski, who noticed a locally caught female corn in a Cape Coral, Florida (on the lower southwest coast) pet shop that exhibited enhanced yellow. The snake was essentially normal with a flush of straw yellow around reddish-brown blotches. He immediately recognized the potential of using it to start selectively breeding to develop a strain of special ultra yellow corns. He has taken these projects through several generations, some of which are addressed later in the 'MIX & MATCH' section under '**Butter**'. In effect he's accelerating the tendency away from orange toward *hyperxanthism*, more yellow than is normally seen in average *Elaphe guttata*.

Rich's F1 offspring from crosses of the original snake to a 'snow', and later to an amelanistic, produced all normal offspring. This was reasonable evidence that the original yellowish female was heterozygous for neither type A anerythrism nor amelanism. When those F1 siblings were crossed, a handful of amelanistics resulted, some of which displayed somewhat enhanced yellow. When those corns were bred to produce an F2 generation, hatchlings initially assumed to be anerythristic and 'snow' corns were among the neonates. The anerythristics tended toward brown instead of black, and the yellow pigment filled in slowly (as it usually does in young corns) to eventually show particularly intensely and attractively in this morph. These are now known as '**Caramel**' corns. The snows got much yellower too, later being recognized as '**Butter**' corns. There seems to be some kind of new gene involved here that mimics, or possibly overshadows anerythrism in some ways, but has also proven to be neither of the known forms of anerythrism, type A nor '**Charcoal**'. It is inherited as a simple recessive gene and is currently under further intense scrutiny as part of many ongoing breeding projects to uncover the true nature of its identity and the range of its "uses" in herpetoculture.

'LAVENDER'

'**Lavender**' is an oddly colored corn in which a pinkish-purple-grey pattern is displayed against a paler greyish-white, making it superficially look like a more attractive variation of anerythrism. In 1985 Rich Zuchowski hatched the first 'lavender' corn as a single animal of an F2 clutch from a female that died egg-bound. The grandparents were a 'snow' corn bred to a wild-caught normal corn from the Sarasota-Punta Gorda area of Florida's lower west coast. It looked like a sort-of-normal baby corn at first, leading his wife, Connie, to christen it '**Mocha**' to describe its slightly unusual chocolate brown appearance *as a hatchling*. It proceeded to slowly change by losing the warmer reddish tones as it grew. This is almost the reverse of what happens in anerythristic corns when they get old and sometimes start turning a browner tone as reds and/or yellows slowly accumulate. The name '**Lavender**' more accurately describes adults and has since emerged as the most universally accepted term after a lively debate raged for a year over the Internet about its heritage.

As the gene was spread to other collectors hidden in some normal looking 'by-products' of other projects, its latent variability resurfaced in John Albrecht's and Dan Thomasco's breedings. They include backgrounds that often show an orangish to pinkish tone in the prettiest specimens, and the dorsal blotching sometimes takes on a purplish to grayish cast.

This baby 'Striped' corn hatched from eggs laid by a wild-caught specimen at a dealer's shop in Tampa, Florida in 1980. Note how the stripe breaks up into a series of dashes closer to the tail.

Striping looks best when the lines are perfectly parallel, clearly delineated, and contrast sharply with the ground color as they do in this amelanistic 'Striped' corn.

When isolated bits of the background appear as circles down the back of 'Motley' corns, the name 'Hurricane' corn has been applied to them.

Efforts are underway to breed banded corns with single big wrap-around saddles that absorb the side blotches and reach from belly to belly across the snakes' backs. *Photo by Don Soderberg and Ryan Moss*

Some lavenders from the start of the project have had eerily attractive red eyes that almost glow with an inner light. This point was missed at first and only later noticed by Jeff Yohe and brought to the attention of Rich about his snakes. Recent reports have shown that it seems to be inherited separately from '**Lavender**' since it has shown up in 'ghost' corns too. The '**Ruby-eye**' trait's pink cast is amplified when combined in the same animal with recessive hypomelanism. This may prove to be the first trait that specifically targets only the eyes for its color effect.

CALICO (PIEBALDISM)

Piebaldism is a generic term for abnormal pigmentation which results in variously sized white areas replacing part of the usual color and pattern. In some individuals the white areas may dominate most of the body, leaving only tiny telltale spots and flecks of red, yellow, and black. Other specimens display unusually enlarged white borders to the dorsal blotches with additional scattered unpigmented splotches over their lengths.

Piebaldism was first noticed by us in a female specimen of *Elaphe guttata* in the private collection of Dwain Collings of Tucson, Arizona in the mid 1980s. It was reputedly collected in the Florida Keys. The white blotches did not cover more than about ten percent of its body as best as we recall. It produced some normal-looking F1 offspring, which were raised and bred together and back to the mother in a cooperative venture between us and Bern Bechtel, among others, during the 1980s. Both of our efforts resulted in only normal-looking progeny after two years of crossing the "hopeful gene carriers" amongst themselves. As the trait appeared not to be heritable, we gave up and dispersed the "hopeful hets" as just captive-bred normal corns. It seemed to be a potentially exciting trait that just wasn't meant to be. At least that's what everyone thought at that point...

Jillian Cowles in Arizona continued the project longer than anyone else, eventually demonstrating with some of her F2 generation that a built-in time delay of two to three years exists before the piebald effect starts to manifest itself. When it finally did, white splotches appeared, sometimes gradually, but other times immediately, like the switching on of a light when the skin was shed. It has virtually always been accompanied by a blistering distortion of the scales at those sites that seems to be a function of the pigment disruption process. This has even occurred in non-piebald offspring of that bloodline, which leaves hope that it can be bred out of the strain to leave healthy corns with only the highly variable color anomaly intact. The delayed onset of the whitening until after maturation, combined with the fact that it has occurred mostly in females, curiously parallels the effects of a human condition called lupus, including its occasional fatal results. Jillian and Tim Rainwater are currently working on further breedings to attempt to separate the color mutation from the deleterious aspects of this strain.

Tim refers to corns of this strain of piebaldism as '**Calico**' to avoid confusion with a new and unrelated corn that he hopes to establish over the next few years. The new piebald is a 1998 hatchling derived from 'bloodred' and anerythristic parental stock, neither of which showed any hint of the bizarre anomaly adorning the creature that hatched. The baby snake at the root of this separate discussion has a singular clearish-white patch approximately one inch long extending completely around its body about midway along its length; the rest is normal in color and pattern. Unfortunately this young female also has several body kinks which may or may not be connected to the color aberration genetically. This is the '**Piebald**' corn being pre-promoted on Tim's list and website. The normal siblings, both parents, and hopefully this animal itself (eventually) are being purposely inbred to bring out this interesting new trait in snakes not beleaguered by muscular or skeletal deformities. Tim is encouraged by the fact that a type of piebaldism that strongly resembles this baby corn's condition already exists in a completely unrelated taxon in ball pythons, *Python regius*, in which it's been reliably demonstrated to be passed on recessively. The challenge of this project embodies the spirit of modern herpetoculture.

One other new corn snake anomaly has come to our attention quite recently. In 1996 Joe Hiduke and Bill Brant hatched two male 'snow' corns that have small, scattered patches of pure red emerging randomly over their bodies. These '**Ruby freckled**' corns resulted unexpectedly from the routine mating of two standard snow corns. As hatchlings they looked like typical snow corns – plain white and translucent - and only started developing a few red scales after a couple skin sheds had occurred. The size of the red spots has slowly increased, sometimes in random clusters, leading Joe and Bill to retain the snakes so progress of the transformation could be monitored. Both males matured in 1998 and fathered offspring for the first time. They have been extremely hardy and healthy, and have shown no evidence of any scalation defects in the red areas or elsewhere. The genetics and degrees of eventual red coverage in this morph are still in the infancy of study. Mention of them is included here purely because of their obvious, but 'reverse,' resemblance to the cases of piebaldism discussed above.

A slightly different variation on striping is shown in this young Emory's rat seen in the late 1970s before people were concentrating so heavily on breeding new morphs. What eventually became of this animal, or whether it ever reproduced, is not known.

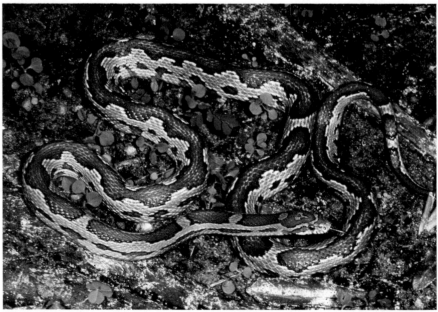

This normally colored corn is exhibiting a clean-cut zigzag pattern that seemingly wants to be a wide stripe made of connected blotches in some places along its back.

The enhanced yellow of 'Caramel' corns is easy to observe on this motley patterned version in which less melanin is evident to mask it over the snake's entire body. *Photo by Rich Zuchowski*

'Aztec' is the name given to this extremely asymmetrical, linear-oriented disruption of the dorsal pattern in some zigzag corns.

PATTERN MUTATIONS

Coloration is only one aspect of a corn snake's appearance. Completely separate sets of genes control how the markings on both the back and belly will be shaped. These genes are subject to the same selective influences as color, making pattern the second major trait undergoing modification at the creative hands of both Mother Nature and herpetoculturists. Three types of pattern anomalies exist in *Elaphe guttata* that we are aware of at present.

'MOTLEY' / 'STRIPED'

'**Motley**' is an inherited anomaly that tends to elongate and join the dorsal blotches together. They can range in appearance from a ladder-like pattern of fused or partially fused blotches to a complete and perfectly even stripe down the entire dorsal surface of the snake. The results can be *extremely variable!* It's not unusual for the pattern to form stretches of partial stripes that meld into normal or partially fused blotches at random areas across the back. The pattern disruption also affects the side blotches, basically erasing or absorbing them, or at least reducing them to scattered remnants of spots and streaks laterally. This mutation also exerts a secondary influence in which the black ventral checkerboarding pattern is completely, or nearly completely, lost. Some specimens will have various shades of reds and oranges present on the belly; others are plain white with a light peppering.

The '**Motley**' mutation cropped up spontaneously in many collections in the early to mid 1980s. Its origins seem to be in wild-caught corns from scattered localities, mostly along the lower west coast of Florida, especially around Hillsborough, Pinellas, Manatee, and Sarasota counties where *E. guttata* occurs in great abundance, and at least once in a specimen from Adel, Georgia. Most notable, and possibly also the earliest among them, was a hatchling female obtained by Dr. Bern Bechtel in 1972. He proved the trait inheritable in 1977 by backcrossing F1 offspring (the product of a normal male bred to the original odd female) back to the mother, resulting in over half the litter exhibiting the aberration, as would be expected if it was passed as a simple recessive trait. It eventually gave rise to a line of snakes in which the latent variability of the anomaly was soon determined through inbreeding trials. The popular name is an abbreviated version of "motley mutant", a term coined by Dr. Bechtel to describe this unpredictably diverse aberration. The motley gene was probably spread far and wide in the meantime since many attractive specimens from that area subsequently entered the pet trade through several herp dealers operating in the Tampa Bay region.

Striping in corn snakes gives the appearance of a wide pale orange line down the centerline of the back, with narrow darker red ones flanking it. A second pair of darker lateral stripes is often present too, but they're usually less distinct, and often broken into short dashes. The dorsal blotches are absent, although vestiges of them often occur on the tail, and less frequently interspersed in the striped pattern on other parts of the body. Completely (100%) dorsally striped examples arc rare, but they exist. The black ventral checkerboard pattern also disappears when this trait occurs.

The first known '**Striped**' corns were hatched by Mike Nolan in England in the mid 1980s. Ernie Wagner imported the original parental stock and some of the striped babies into the U.S. He continued the breeding project and spread the morph widely in the U.S. Low fertility in the males, and failure to thrive of some hatchlings has plagued the strain, prompting many breeders to outcross striped corns to many other morphs. This has led to interesting new combinations of traits while also strengthening the bloodline by incorporating the theory of hybrid vigor - introducing fresh healthy genes to an apparently overly inbred population. Mark Bell is one of the people who has worked extensively at this; his striped amelanistics were the first to be produced as part of his efforts in this direction.

Although '**Striped**' and '**Motley**' corns breed true in the sense that they don't produce normally patterned offspring when bred together, they don't always beget babies with as unusual patterns as the parents. Furthermore, striped and motley have proven to be related to each other. Crossing the two together produces 100% oddly-patterned offspring ranging in looks from long-blotched "barely motley" to fully striped. The one constant was that all lacked the ventral checkerboard pattern. This suggests that '**Striped**' and '**Motley**' may both be *alleles* (versions of the same gene) and are codominant when they exist together in the same animal. This means that either one alone is recessive when paired with a gene for normal corn snake pattern. But when the pair of pattern genes present in a corn are some combination of the '**Motley**' and/or '**Striped**' alleles, they'll be expressed as either '**Motley**', '**Striped**', or a mixture of the two. We and others have made crosses to test this many times since 1991 when Mike McEachern suggested the possibility. Thus, '**Striped**' and '**Motley**' corns appear to be different versions of the same trait genetically.

'Motley', which we'll assume to include 'striped' from here on, may hold the greatest potential for continued experimentation to produce new designer morphs of corn snakes in the future. One that's already earned a trade name is the '**Cubed**' corn in which the central dorsal stripe is broken into a series of well-defined, square-edged rectangular blotches. When neatly isolated small circles are all that's left of the background between the connected blotches; we've heard it marketed as '**Hurricane**' corn. The adjective '**Pastel**' is catching on as a prefix name for motleys whenever a significant amount of pinkish-orange coloration develops between their blotches.

A '**Banded**' pattern alteration in corns is currently being developed. It relies, at least in some cases, on the introduction of the 'motley' gene, and maybe on a distant *emoryi* heritage in other cases. In it the usual squarish or rectangular dorsal blotches expand sideways to form wrap-

The 'Snow' corn was the first widely-bred double recessive trait. Its obvious extreme divergence from the colors of normal corns caught the public's fancy nearly two decades ago.

The prevalence of pinkish tones on and between the blotches has resulted in the trade name 'Bubblegum snow' corn for specimens such as this.

As with all kinds of corns, ample variation exists even among 'Snow' corns for specialty morphs within that trait to emerge such as this yellow-blotched phase. The blotches appear with a more greenish tinge in other individuals, making the name 'Green-blotched snow' show up on price lists occasionally.

'Butter' corns are living proof that plenty of yellow is lurking under all the red and black of some strains of corns. They may also have a gene that actually enhances the amount and/or distribution of yellow pigment. No *E. g. emoryi* bloodlines were involved in its creation.

around, saddle-like markings that resemble elongated ovals draped across the snakes' backs. The eventual goal is a corn snake with cleanly defined crossbands reaching from the ventral plates completely across the back in a series all the way down snakes' lengths, much like some of the ringed milk snakes (*Lampropeltis triangulum*). '**Saddleback**' is an alternative name also used for this look. Combining the banded pattern with the color attributes of his '**Milk snake phase**' corns is one direction that Rich Zuchowski has sought to enhance the appealing effect that mimics true milk snakes of the northeastern U.S. Don Soderberg's crosses with '**Miami phase**' corns have taken the project down a related path toward a high contrast corn with bands boldly standing out from the ground color.

'ZIGZAG' / 'ZIPPER'

One source of this phenomenon was begun inadvertently in 1984 as a byproduct from our project involving normally-patterned corns, one being our original '**Charcoal**' female from Pine Island, Florida. As we inbred for a few generations to investigate that new morph, we also noticed an increasing number of offspring with fused blotches. A few exhibited longer stretches of zigzaggy blotches that resembled a zipper. More accurately, it looks as if the usual squarish mid-dorsal blotches had been split lengthwise and partially slid apart forward and backward, but remained attached at the corners. Pairing the most extreme examples soon got us offspring with up to 95% zigzagged patterns. They do not breed 100% true in the same sense that simple recessive traits produce when bred together. But the more extreme specimens have generally produced a higher percentage of zigzags per litter and individual specimens with larger percentages of the connected pattern on them than less extreme specimens do. Normally patterned hatchlings still appear from time to time in the line too; they are especially prevalent when crossing normally patterned descendents of zigzags that would have been expected to be heterozygous for the trait. This suggests that the mode of inheritance is not so simple and is far from being clearly understood to date.

Rich Zuchowski has a somewhat divergent form in which the dorsal design is broken up into an unpredictable pattern of irregular blotching, streaks, and spots. He has coined the name '**Aztec**' for it. It is a asymmetrical pattern of a different line of zigzags pioneered by John Albrecht as an offshoot of his work with the lavender corn project. We have since seen some of our zigzags diverge toward the unpredictable chaos of the aztec design too, leading us to suspect that the same gene may be at work in both forms. Andy Barr is also working with another (different?) line of 'zigzaggy' corn in which a very distinct, thick, wavy stripe undulates down the midline of the dorsum. It actually appears as a cleaner, more well-defined version that's bound to be popular in the future. It was created at least in part from our original '**Zigzag**' strain crossed out to unrelated stock.

What may turn into a new pattern anomaly of the future is displayed by Don Soderberg's '**Chocolate**' Emory's rat, discussed earlier under anerythrism. A high percentage of its dorsal blotches appear split apart diagonally, running down its entire length as a nearly parallel row of alternating smaller spots that are virtually the same size as the lateral blotches. That '**Spotted**' effect has been inherited in the expected simple recessive mode along with the chocolate color aberration it first appeared with. It wouldn't be hard to imagine them as a zigzag pattern if they were just slightly connected, but maybe this new look will prove to be different entirely. Color variants heavily outnumber pattern variants in corns, so something new like this on the herpetocultural horizon is welcomed!

PLAIN BELLY

The absence of the ventral pattern of black geometric checkerboarding is less conspicuous than dorsal pattern abnormalities but has shown up in at least two morphs of corns independently. While the amount of ventral coverage by normal black markings can vary considerably between individuals in nature, the simple fact of whether or not it's present at all seems to be genetically controlled as an all or nothing trait. This seems to be a simple recessive in the case of bloodreds where the lack of belly blotching is clearly inherited independently of the eventual degree of unicolor dorsal redness in adults. Intriguingly, we've had *some* offspring from 'bloodred' X normal crosses that also lack virtually all of their checkerboarding pattern or have it reduced to mere hints of normal checkerboarding concentrated along the edges of their ventrals, leaving the centers of their bellies essentially clear. But in motleys/stripeds, the patternless ventrum *only* occurs accompanying the dorsal anomaly, no matter to what degree it's expressed. We have never seen a plain belly in a heterozygous 'motley' corn. Furthermore, offspring between '**Bloodreds**' and '**Motleys**' have normally patterned ventrums indicating that the plain belly trait is non-allelic between the two anomalies.

Pattern anomalies can also affect the ventrum. These four corns' bellies exemplify commonly seen variations ranging from squared-off bold checkerboarding on the white background of 'Okeetees', less distinct checks on the orange-white of typical corns, the lack of black on the heavily red-infused belly of a 'Bloodred', to the plain white ventrum of a 'Striped' corn.

Just as in a blizzard, all you see is white in the 'Blizzard' corn. Actually, minute traces of yellow sometimes creep into their patterns with age. The clear patches on this hatchling are caused by water between the layers of its skin just prior to shedding.

The 'Pearl' corn seems to have reached the 'blizzard' corn look through use of the 'Lavender' bloodline instead of the 'Charcoal's' to eliminate the reds and yellows. It's also possible that other 'mysterious' factors are involved too. *Photo by Tim Rainwater*

'Amber' corns are a combination of two recessive traits, caramel and hypomelanism.

Freshly-hatched 'Bloodred' corns have gray heads and weak to non-existent black blotch borders, subtle hints of the change to come.

MIXING and MATCHING

The preceding color and pattern variants exist as singular traits, are reproduced following simple genetics, and already are involved in ongoing selective breeding efforts. Undoubtedly more new ones will surface to spice the number of variations possible in the near future. A few that we should expect are anomalies reducing yellow and red pigmentation on a par with hypomelanism. And possibly someone will find the opposite hyper versions (having abnormally excessive amounts of all those pigments). The latter may already be here in 'Bloodred' (with red) and 'Caramel' corns (with yellow). New heritable traits like these are eagerly being sought to expand the number of paints on modern herpetoculturists' palettes.

Besides waiting for new aberrations to pop up and hoping that they're heritable, new corn morphs may be created artificially by combining two or more existing traits. 'Snow' corns, presently the most familiar double recessive mutation, got the trend rolling initially not long after their second basic ingredient, type A anerythrism, appeared to make it possible. The desire to expand the mixing and matching is well underway today within thousands of collections worldwide. Fanciful names for the newly created phenotypes are being applied at a rate that makes it nearly impossible to stay current on them all and fully describe their genetics. Most of these new cultivars will be winnowed out as they fail to withstand the "Hatband Test" of popularity over time, but a few will manage to pass the test. Those will ultimately stick as a loyal following accepts them and strives to further intensify or otherwise change and improve the strain. Some that seem destined to last, or some that just caught our eye, are illustrated in photos and/or briefly described below:

'SNOW' CORNS

'Snow' corns were the first "white" snakes, and at the same time were the first double recessive snakes in history that were *purposely* created in captivity. It was accomplished by the logical experimental step of combining the recessive genes for amelanism and anerythrism into one individual. When those traits occur simultaneously, neither black nor red pigments are present. That leaves only the iridophores and maybe some residual yellows to color the snake, creating an essentially white specimen that still retains enough remaining subtle pigments to delineate the pattern easily. This came as somewhat of a surprise to the two creators, Glen Slemmer and Bern Bechtel, who weren't quite sure what to expect in the mid 1970s when both men strove to achieve the same results independently of one another; Slemmer won the race by a year.

They started the experiment by crossing an amelanistic corn with a type A anerythristic corn, which produced all normal-looking offspring. Those babies from the first round of the breeding effort are called the F1 (first filial) generation. Each F1 juvenile carries both recessive traits, paired with a normal gene that they inherited from the parent that carried the normal gene governing that particular trait. These babies are double heterozygous because they carry forms of two different mutated genes. You can't tell this just by looking at their phenotype (outward physical appearance) since all look like normal baby corns. Breeding these F1 offspring together produces the F2 generation. The genes of the F1 snakes segregate and assort into new combinations in the F2 babies. Some babies look normal, others lack either black or red like a grandparent, and a few lack both black and red pigments.

This is most easily shown by using a simple graph called a Punnett square to imagine how a clutch of 16 eggs might look at hatching. The expected F1 cross results in an F2 generation with approximately one out of every sixteen snakes lacking red and black pigments at the same time. That one baby is a snow corn which may grow up to be a pearly creature sporting a white background and blotches varying from flesh, ivory, pink, yellow, or greenish. The remaining 15 hatchlings of the imaginary clutch will exhibit either of the other mutations of the grandparents, or will appear normal, and occur at a ratio of three amelanistics, three anerythristics, and nine normal-looking neonates. However, some of the 15 'non-snows' will also carry one or both of the recessive genes that are not visually apparent. It will be impossible to discover their genotype (true genetic makeup) without future breeding trials to prove their genetic heritage.

Breeders have already started marketing the most extreme forms such as the **'Green-blotched snow,'** in which the dorsal blotches exhibit a yellowish-green tinge that is probably a result of interplay between light and the poorly understood reflective cell layer in most snakes' skins. A **'Bubblegum snow'** is also being refined to emphasize the pink tones in the otherwise white background. They may be analogous to the **'Strawberry snow'** being bred and marketed in England by Kevin Stevens.

Until a few years ago, all **'Snow'** corns were derived from the common type A anerythrism. Inevitably, **'Charcoals'** (type Bs) were bred into the strain by Rich Zuchowski, Jack Cole, Art Meyer, and us just to see how it might differ, if at all. The 'Charcoal' corns lack of yellow had the rather dramatic effect of virtually eliminating whatever delineated the blotches on snow corns, thus they appeared plain white. We dubbed this phase the **'Blizzard'** corn - as in a blizzard, all you see is white. Alas, not all specimens grew up to be quite as pure white as we had hoped. Some examples still retained a trace of a yellow ring where the blotch would have been, whereas others possessed a faint shadow pattern only visible in strong light. It was almost as if a small dog had wandered through to soil the blizzard's purity! These tendencies toward yellowing aren't apparent in neonates because of the delay in yellow's formation in corns.

We mustn't forget the fact that even our original Pine Island female was apparently heterozygous for type A anerythrism, which may somehow be responsible for the lingering yellow of some 'Blizzard' corns, or any

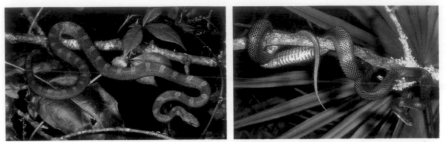

'Bloodred' corns slowly turn into solid red snakes as they mature, but are also quite attractive at the intermediate stages when the dorsal blotches can still be easily counted. As adults, 'Bloodreds' of about five years of age or more appear as deep solid red creatures with little or no trace of pattern, including having no black ventral spots.

The 'Crimson' corn is a beefed-up 'Miami phase' corn that's also hypomelanistic. Efforts to emphasize the boldness of the red blotches against the pale ground color are heightened by "wiping the slate clean of dirty wash" through the addition of the hypo gene. *Photo by Rich Zuchowski*

The name 'Ghost' corn was inspired by how the colors seemed to be "spirited away" by the effects of type A anerythrism and hypomelanism. The faded black remaining is indicative of how much melanin is removed by the latter trait, often a difficult thing to imagine when viewing a basic hypomelanistic corn that has its red pigment intact.

other consequences of crosses it may have inadvertently participated in.

Apparently another strain of white corn was also investigated (created?) by John Albrecht and existed in at least two variations dubbed '**Pink snow**' and '**White snow.**' Both are offshoots of the '**Lavender**' (mocha) corn line of Rich Zuchowski's. The pink line looks like what might be expected from crossing amelanism and lavender, highlighting a rosy pink tinge. The other 'white' line is a more or less pure white corn snake that may be a triple homozygous concoction combining lavender, amelanism, and type A anerythrism, and may be what's been referred to as a '**Pearl**' corn. It shouldn't be confused with another recessive trait called *leucism*, which obliterates all color *and pattern.* The bright white strain of leucistic Texas rat snakes *Elaphe obsoleta lindheimeri* is the best known form of this rare trait today. Like true melanism, leucism has not occurred in *Elaphe guttata* yet to the best of our current knowledge. Still, some specimens of blizzard and pearl corns become extremely white.

In researching the histories of many different morphs of corns for this book, a cloud of uncertainty blew in about the various kinds of anerythrism and their roles in some of the multi-recessive morphs. It's best to tackle the uncertainties after first digesting the discussions of the other corn morphs involving anerythrism that follow. See *"Corn Soup"* at the end of the INTERGRADATION & HYBRIDIZATION section.

'BUTTER'

When '**Caramel**' is combined with amelanism, the result is a corn that appears to be a hyperxanthic '**Snow**' corn with golden yellow covering most of its body as an adult. Hatchlings start out rather white like baby snows. That is to be expected since the intensity and bodily distribution of yellow pigment is never very apparent until any corn reaches at least a few months to a year in age. An adult resembles the most intensely yellow of '**Creamsicle**' corns, but brighter, and without the tendency to lean towards peachy oranges like '**Creamsicles**' often do. Unlike '**Creamsicles**', these corns are *not* a subspecific cross involving the western race of corn snake, *L. g. emoryi*. Rich Zuchowski has christened his creation with the new trade name '**Butter**' corn.

'AMBER'

The '**Caramel**' high-yellow trait combined with hypomelanism produces corns ranging from a golden amber to a pleasing light greenish brown. By softening the masking influence of the black, the yellow wash is much more evident. This appears to be an ideal animal in which to acquire two interesting genes that have not yet been used to mix and match into all the other corn morphs yet.

'BLOODRED'

'**Bloodred**' corns ('**blood corns**' is a shortened version of the name sometimes applied to them) are an interesting morph that falls somewhere between a wild one and a designer morph of captivity. They were originally developed by Ed Leach in the 1970s and 80s, beginning with snakes he found in an area north of the city of Palatka in northeastern Florida. Many corns from there tend to be somewhat unicolor as adults *already* - red blotches on a red-orange background – which attracted him to experiment with them further. Certain specimens had exceptionally pretty, brilliant red coloration with reduced black borders around the blotches. In many, the lateral blotches are all but invisible. The tendency for the ground color to match the blotch color may be a form of *hypererythrism* (an abnormally excessive amount of red pigment), although it is inherited variably from individual to individual, not like a simple recessive trait.

When Ed inbred his early precursor '**Bloodred**' stock, many offspring totally lacked the black ventral checkerboarding. They also displayed an intense and unicolor red dorsal coloration, extremely diminished black blotch outlines, and loss of the associated lateral blotching. The lack, or virtual total lack, of ventral pattern seemed to be a simple recessive trait early in the breeding efforts, although we have started seeing evidence of it in out-crossed corns more recently. The quality of the dorsal color and pattern and reduction of black outlining, on the other hand, occurred in every gradation of all the possibilities within the group, rather than as all-or-nothing traits. The two traits are not always completely linked - we have seen some out-crossed individuals that showed evidence of their '**Bloodred**' heritage dorsally but did not inherit the lack of ventral pattern. However, it is generally accepted that both traits must be present for the animal to be designated as a traditional '**Bloodred**' corn in the herp trade. It's also possible that more than two genes, not necessarily inherited as simple recessive genes, or multiple alleles of some genes, are involved in the inheritance of this complicated association of traits.

Since its creation, the strain has been out-crossed into amelanistic, anerythristic, hypomelanistic, and several other non-related bloodlines, as well as inbred to continue the pure strain. It should prove handy in intensifying the reds of other strains that haven't yet been explored much, analogous to the opportunities the 'caramel' corn line offers with yellow. Sometimes this mixing produces heightened red in some offspring that could no longer be deemed pure '**Bloodreds**', but turned out to be unusually beautiful in their own right, as Pat and Jerry Loll have frequently brought to our envious attention over the years. Outcrossing usually dilutes the purity of the solid red, so large numbers of offspring must be raised and the best selected for further crossing for preserving (reintensifying) the original redness.

The purebred '**Bloodred**' strain tends to produce large clutches (often 30+) of small eggs and small hatchlings that are sometimes difficult to get started feeding voluntarily. Some finicky feeders want to start out

This large male 'Pewter' corn took on a more unicolor gray coloration the older it became just as bloodreds get redder with age. Pewter is a combination of 'Bloodred' and 'Charcoal' in the same snake.

We're not sure exactly how to classify the frosted look in corns. It adds a distinctive whitish speckling effect to the whole snake by concentrating the pigment of each scale to the central keel.

on lizards or not eat at all. Out-crossing is succeeding in strengthening the line and persuading higher percentages of neonates to voluntarily accept pinkie mice as first meals.

'CRIMSON'

This is a "new and improved" cultivar of '**Miami phase**' corns by Rich Zuchowski. To brighten and clean up the red-orange blotches and the silvery ground color, hypomelanism was bred in to reduce the dirty wash of melanin over the entire body, while retaining enough for delineation of the blotches.

'GHOST'

Combining hypomelanism and anerythrism produces a pale snake that exhibits a ghostly, faded image of a normal corn. Many display delicate shades of lavender, pink, and yellow, enhanced and deepened by the contrasting grayish outlines in the pattern. The subtler tones that some individuals develop will show only after several months or more of age. Although we first created the original 'ghost' corns using only type A anerythrism, we realize that others have introduced charcoal to hypomelanism to come up with similarly colored specimens. Their genetic ancestry will become increasingly hard to track as many people, including us, are already having difficulty distinguishing them by looks alone.

'PEWTER'

The resulting combination of '**Bloodred**' and '**Charcoal**' yields a medium grey snake with dorsal blotches that fade into the nearly identical ground color in adults. The dorsal blotches lose their well-defined edges with age until large adults exhibit a cryptically blurred pattern that's almost hidden against the ground color. Some specimens exhibit a fine "dusting" of black, inciting the alternate name '**Pepper**' corn for this double recessive trait.

'FROSTED'

We've tucked this trait here for sheer lack of certainty about how to categorize it properly. The effect we've seen in several specimens of different colorations is for a pale speckling or highlighting to whiten the scales, particularly inside the dorsal blotches. The resulting frosty look adds a contrasting wash-over that's distinctive. One strain has its origins in the Tampa, Florida region nearly two decades ago when some crosses were made between Mike Falcon, Andy Barr, and Jack Cole's corns. It involved an odd locally-caught snake that was at first suspected of being a hybrid cross between a corn and a yellow rat snake *E. o. quadrivittata*. It was crossed to a '**Snow**'corn that apparently also carried hypomelanism in the first generation of experimental breeding. It now appears that the mystery snake was not a hybrid, but instead an early hypomelanistic corn unrecognized at the time. The frosted look may be a product of its interaction with other recessive color reductions, but it's not yet fully clear how this trait intermingles and is inherited. To further complicate the issue, back during this same period a grey rat *E. o. spiloides* was separately bred to the same male '**Snow**' corn, and also resulted in viable young sporting a similar frosty appearance. Some of this line was distributed before it was eventually retired in favor of the other "pure" *guttata* strain. The pictures and living specimens we've examined bear an uncanny resemblance to stone-washed corns mentioned earlier.

INTERGRADATION & HYBRIDIZATION

The nominate race of corn snakes *Elaphe guttata guttata* **intergrades** with the Great Plains rats *Elaphe guttata emoryi* west of the Mississippi River. Intergrades occur naturally where different subspecies of the same species meet geographically, and those animals breed together to throw offspring resembling the parents and everything in-between them in looks. There are no serious biological barriers to prevent this from happening. Crossing individuals of the species *Elaphe guttata* from New Jersey, Florida, Utah, and Mexico in captivity is still making intergrades, even if they would have never come in contact in the wild under normal circumstances. We think of this phenomenon, tagged *forced intergradation*, as a byproduct of our modern-day ability to bring far-ranging races of corn snakes together for experimental herpetocultural crosses.

Hybrids result from the mating of different species, technically an impossibility if the strict definition of species – a group of organisms which interbreeds, but is reproductively isolated from all other similar groups - is adhered to and believed to be infallible. Crosses between *Elaphe guttata* and yellow rat snakes *Elaphe obsoleta quadrivittata* have occurred in the wild and in captivity. Additionally, black rats *E. o. obsoleta* and Baird's rats *E. o. bairdi* (or just *Elaphe bairdi*) have produced viable offspring with corns in collections.

Corns have also been tricked into copulating with other colubrid snake species and genera. One method involves switching prospective mates at the frenzied height of sexual excitement just prior to a normal intraspecies breeding. The interspecific crosses that we are aware of so far are with rat snakes *Elaphe obsoleta*. Intergeneric crosses we've seen are with western gopher snakes (*Pituophis melanoleucus catenifer*), California king snakes (*Lampropeltis getula californiae*), gray-banded kings (*Lampropeltis alterna*), and milk snakes (*Lampropeltis triangulum*); the subspecies *campbelli, sinaloae, annulata,* and *nelsoni*). Interestingly, the gene for amelanism in *L. t. nelsoni* is apparently related to the amelanistic gene of corns. This was proven when albinism appeared in several offspring of an F1 cross between an amelanistic corn and a Nelson's milk heterozygous for its own presumed separate form of amelanism. It's not uncommon for intergeneric matings to result in partially infertile clutches of eggs, or for the offspring that do hatch to be sterile or less fertile reproducers themselves.

CORN SOUP – *Challenges Beyond the Basics for Tomorrow's Herpetoculturists*

In poring over the case histories of all these morphs of corns, a curious connection has become apparent. The '**Lavender**' strain behind the '**Pink snow**', '**White snow**' and '**Pearl**' corn (discussed earlier in the section on '**Snow**' / '**Blizzard**' corns) was descended from an ancestor from coastal southwest Florida. This is essentially the same region of origin of our original Pine Island female corn that introduced '**Charcoal**' (type B anerythrism) that went on to make '**Blizzards**', and our '**Zigzags**'. Most of the early, more common **type A anerythristic** specimens also came from southwest Florida. The conundrum compounds: The '**Caramel**' line, whose original purveyor was also from that same geographical area, seems to carry a new gene affecting red / yellow pigment that's interacting 'weirdly' with other known *guttata* morphs.

Southwest Florida seems to be a recurring link in all these cases. Can these facts somehow be parts of the same puzzle? Could a new mutant gene (or genes) exist that's actually widespread in populations of corns from a broad portion of lower coastal southwest Florida – one that's crept into collections via several avenues to leave us presently confused? Is it recessive too or just hidden by the other colors we're tossing into the stew before we know what we really have? Could it be something affecting those iridophores ("reflective cells") that we haven't mentioned since the opening comments on amelanistic corns, or is it something else entirely?

Not to purposely confuse the issue, the '**Caramel**' corn history in particular is interesting in a related way since it's been proven that some caramel corns are in fact heterozygous for type A anerythrism, which was introduced back with the first breeding of the original yellowish '**Caramel**' female to a male '**Snow**'corn by Rich Zuchowski. This is analogous to the situation with his lavender corn line, and is also, non-coincidentally, the case with our own charcoal corn in which we too chose a male snow corn in the first mating to explore its heritage.

The early introduction of known recessive ingredients, such as type A anerythrism, has seemingly clouded our ability to decipher the exact "recipes" of some of the new morphs popping up a decade or more later. While it will continue to complicate our understanding of the genetic heritage of some emerging corn snake lines, there was a purpose to the original madness. The using of '**Snow**' corns as initial mates was a sort of litmus test *at the time* to see if newfound snakes were exhibiting (in disguised form), or were carrying genes for the aberrant traits already familiar to us. Since there were not nearly as many different traits around in the mid 1980s as there are today, the two common ones, amelanism and type A anerythrism, were easiest to test for by simply crossing a snow corn to the newcomer. Then their F1 offspring were backcrossed a couple years later to observe what turned up in the F2 generation.

Using totally normal-looking corns from distant origins as first mates, so as to avoid specimens possibly heterozygous for the traits we were investigating, would have *also* been nice to do as a back-up strategy. We both might have exercised that option *too*, except for the fact that all three original corns that got us working with the three morphs noted above were females. Had they been males, they could have been crossed out to multiple females, including normals *and* '**Snows**', allowing us to gauge the phenotypic and genotypic effects and relationships with other morphs sooner.

Despite which experimental path was chosen then, the fundamental point to be made here is the necessity to determine whether "new" corns suddenly showing up are really new genetically, or just *look* different. This is particularly relevant today since many corn morphs haven't been around long enough yet to be seen in all their myriad forms. It reminds us of those fabled blind men feeling and describing different parts of the elephant, thinking they are 'seeing' the whole picture. In the meantime, more and more herp hobbyists are jumping the gun and tagging new names on slightly divergent specimens of pre-existing morphs. Some do it in the zeal to 'create' something new and coin a name; others are dominated by the fervor to gain commercial marketing advantages. Without the benefit of having tested the "new" traits in breeding trials with known genetic variants, preferably over several generations, relationships are becoming increasingly hazed.

It's definitely too early to draw any firm conclusions about all the mysteries of *guttata* genetics until some very meticulous soul decides to devote some serious time into unraveling the dynamics of their interwoven genetic relationships. If we get nothing else out of this, it's irrefutable that the lower west coast of Florida has been the source of a number of extraordinary genes in *Elaphe guttata*. Don't forget, that region also gave us **hypomelanism** and '**Motley**' too!

We know that such examples cast a gloomy forecast of the growing confusion in tracing the genealogies of corn snakes, and after only a few decades of human 'guidance'! More chefs will undoubtedly contribute to the mélange as herpetoculture continues to expand. Some have expressed the concern that the end concoction might resemble the same outcome as when we whimsically scribbled all our crayons into one thick, gummy brown smudge – resulting in a nondescript (and not very attractive) corn snake with the appeal of burnt toast. That worry, at least, is unrealistic because mankind's eternal appreciation of and quest for beauty will always cull away from spawning many non-descript 'shades-of-brown' amalgamations.

When agreeing to author this book, we expected it to be a rather simple task of 'rounding up and explaining all the new morphs of corns. It turned out quite differently. It was a sobering experience learning the complexities of what's really happening out there in the hands of a pyramiding number of herpetocultural investigators. It really brought home the realization that the time is ripe for someone to initiate a pedigree documentation system before what's still remembered of the various morphs' origins is lost forever.

APPENDIX

ASSOCIATION of REPTILE and AMPHIBIAN VETERINARIANS – (ARAV)

This international non-profit organization of more than 1300 professionals and interested individuals is devoted to improving herp veterinary care, husbandry, and breeding through education, exchange of ideas, and research. They publish an informative quarterly bulletin, hold annual conferences, and maintain a directory on their website that helps people in need locate herp-savvy vets near their homes across the U.S. and around the world. Membership in ARAV is open to anyone.

Contact info: ARAV, c/o Wilbur Amand, VMD, P.O. Box 605, Chester Heights, Pennsylvania 19017, TEL.: 610-358-9530; FAX: 610-892 4813; EMAIL: 75634.235@compuserve.com; WEBSITE: http://www.arav.org

NATIONAL REPTILE & AMPHIBIAN ADVISORY COUNCIL (NRAAC)

NRAAC is an organization of informed and politically active concerned herpetologists, herpetoculturists and others interested in herpetofauna. Its purpose is to monitor and to prevent legislation or regulations that will be detrimental to the legal keeping and breeding of reptiles and amphibians. It seeks to provide a source of technically accurate and objective herpetological information and advice for guiding policies involving reptiles and amphibians in the U.S. at both state and federal levels. Its additional purpose is to organize the herp community into a cohesive group with the power to implement these goals. Consider joining to help NRAAC do its job for *you!* Contact them on the web at: http://nraac.org , or write to: NRAAC, 508 East Howard Lane, Austin, Texas 78753-9767.

CORN SNAKE PROGENY PREDICTOR

Noel "Mick" Spencer has created a computer program that allows you to plug in data about your *Elaphe guttata* parent stock to predict the expected ratios of color and pattern in their offspring. This will undoubtedly save many people a lot of time and befuddlement in finding fast answers to their questions about "What do I get if I cross...". CORN SNAKE PROGENY PREDICTOR section:

The handy Windows program can be downloaded, free of charge thanks to Mick's generosity, from the Internet at this website: **http://home.epix.net/~nspencer/cornprog.html**

IN PREPARATION: The Biology of the Corn Snake *Elaphe guttata*

This monographic book will be the first comprehensive coverage of the corn snake and its entire subspecies complex, illustrated with detailed distribution maps, line drawings and _hundreds_ of color photographs. Chapters will include: taxonomic status, fossil history, natural history, reproductive behavior, color and pattern mutations, genetics, hybrids and others. Each subspecies account will include detailed descriptions, followed by distribution records and in-depth natural history notes. All chapters will be authored by recognized herpetologists and herpetoculturists experienced with corn snakes in the wild and captivity.

Information, suggestions, and photographs relative to *Elaphe guttata* are welcomed. Contact address: Klaus-Dieter Schulz, Bushmaster Publications, Kaesereistrasse 4, 9305 Berg SG, Switzerland, telephone & fax: +41 71 455 25 69; email: KSelaphe@aol.com _or_ n.helfenberger@bluewin.ch

REFERENCES

Applegate, R. 1992 **The General Care and Maintenance of Milk Snakes**. Advanced Vivarium Systems, Lakeside, California.

Bechtel, H. B. 1978. **Heredity of Pattern Mutation in the Corn Snake, *Elaphe guttata*, Demonstrated in Captive Breedings.** Copeia. 1978 (4):719-721.

Bechtel, H. B. 1989. **Color Mutations in the Corn Snake, *Elaphe guttata guttata* : Review and Additional Breeding Data.** The Journal of Heredity 80(4):273-276.

Bechtel, H. B. 1995 **Reptile and Amphibian Variants – Colors, Patterns, and Scales**. Kreiger Publishing Company, Malabar, Florida.

Kauffeld, C. 1957 **Snakes and Snake Hunting**. Hanover House, Garden City, New York.

Kauffeld, C. 1969 **Snakes: The Keeper and the Kept**. Doubleday & Company, Inc., Garden City, New York.

Klingenberg, R. 1993 **Understanding Reptile Parasites**. Advanced Vivarium Systems, Lakeside, California.

Mader, D. R. (ed.). 1996 **Reptile Medicine and Surgery**. W.B. Saunders Company, Philadelphia, Pennsylvania.

Mattison, C. 1998 **Keeping and Breeding Snakes**. (2nd Fully Revised Edition), Blanford Press, London.

McEachern, M. J. 1991 **A Color Guide to Corn Snakes Captive-Bred in the United States**. Advanced Vivarium Systems, Lakeside, California.

McEachern, M. J. 1991 **Keeping and Breeding Corn Snakes**. Advanced Vivarium Systems, Lakeside, California.

Rossi, J. and R. Rossi. 1996 **What's Wrong With My Snake?** Advanced Vivarium Systems, Lakeside, California.

Schulz, K.-D. 1996 **A Monograph of the Colubrid Snakes of the Genus *Elaphe* Fitzinger**. Koeltz Scientific Books, Czech Republic.

Slavens, F. L. and K. Slavens. 1998 **Reptiles and Amphibians in Captivity - Breeding, Longevity, & Inventory**. Slaveware, Seattle, Washington.

Witwer, M. and Aaron B. **Early Breeding in a Captive Corn Snake *Elaphe guttata guttata*.** Herpetological Review 26(3):141 1995.

Index

Bill & Kathy Love have been keeping and breeding corn snakes since the early 1970s. They maintain a moderately large private herp collection at their home outside Ft. Myers, Florida where continued selective breeding projects are underway. These aspects and sales are carried out under the business name *CornUtopia*, while active pursuits in herpetological photography, writing, and ecotouring are the realms of its sister company, *Blue Chameleon Ventures*. Bill & Kathy are always interested in receiving information about new color and pattern variations emerging in *Elaphe guttata* in addition to other herpetocultural breakthroughs new world records, and other comments that may be useful in future updates of this book. They can be contacted through their Internet website at: http://www.cyberstreet.com/loveherp or by telephone at 941-728-2390. ***Photo by Darya Tchetvergova***

One of our 1999 hatchling albino 'Okeetee' corns displayed an unusually large amount of pure white coloration over it's ground color, an area which is usually a nondescript 'clearish' tone at hatching. It's new things like that which continue to inspire us and other serious breeders, and also fuel the continued development of beautiful variations in the future.